"Want to wake up without buyer's remorse the day after you close on your first home? The priceless information in this handbook for the first-time home buyer can prevent the common pitfalls new home buyers face. It is a comprehensive and essential guide for taking each step of new home ownership with confidence."

— Karen A. Ebert, MPM, RMP, e-Pro, Realtor
Austin Landmark Property Services, Inc. ALPS
karen@alpsmgmt.com

THE FIRST-TIME HOMEOWNER'S HANDBOOK

A Complete Guide and Workbook for the First-Time Home Buyer: With Companion CD-ROM

THE FIRST-TIME HOMEOWNER'S HANDBOOK—A Complete Guide and Workbook for the First-Time Home Buyer: With Companion CD-ROM

ISBN-13: 978-0-910627-70-2   ISBN-10: 0-910627-70-3

Library of Congress Cataloging-in-Publication Data
The first-time homeowner's handbook : a complete guide and workbook for the
first-time home buyer.
     p. cm.
  Includes bibliographical references and index.
  ISBN-13: 978-0-910627-70-2 (alk. paper)
  ISBN-10: 0-910627-70-3
  1. House buying--United States. 2. Mortgage loans--United States. I.
Atlantic Publishing Co.

  HD259.F57 2006
  643'.120973222
                            2006018672
  Printed in the United States

ART DIRECTION & INTERIOR DESIGN: Meg Buchner • megadesn@mchsi.com
BOOK PRODUCTION DESIGN: Cyanotype Book Architects • www.cyanotype.ca

TABLE of CONTENTS

CHAPTER 4   BUILDING YOUR OWN HOUSE   69

CHAPTER 5
UNDERSTANDING THE HOME BUYING PROCESS 101

CHAPTER 6   THE CREDIT REPORT   123

CHAPTER 7
WHERE TO FIND THE BEST FINANCING   155

CHAPTER 8
THE CLOSING—A PRACTICAL VIEW   193

CHAPTER 9   THE NEXT STEPS
FOLLOWING THE PURCHASE OF YOUR HOME   209

APPENDIX A - REAL ESTATE GLOSSARY   219

APPENDIX B - MORTGAGE GLOSSARY   237

f

FIRST TIME HOME BUYER

By Joe Adamaitis

President, Direct Mortgage Services, Inc.

Just five short years ago, who would have imagined that the Internet and bold advertising would have such a huge effect on the way people bought homes? Looking back, no one imagined how four lenders might give you an offer if you simply went online and applied. You never thought that TV ads for mortgage companies every five minutes would begin to have an impact on the way people might apply for mortgages. Who imagined those nasty pop-ups every time you go online showing falling interest rates in all 50 states was not really a lender but a lead generator? For realtors, the same has occurred. Today we have realtors facing off against online companies who sell a borrower a home over the Internet for less commission.

Progress? Maybe.

In some regards these changes are evidence of great innovation and great entrepreneurship. As with all new advancements, there are good things and bad that happen. For first time homebuyers, there are huge rewards for using the Internet to find out as much as possible about buying a home. There are also some pitfalls you will want to avoid.

For instance, the four offers you get for applying online may well work to your benefit, but understand that you have been funneled into only four out of hundreds of lenders for those rates. Consider that these four lenders pay to get your name and information sent to them. And those TV ads that claim that you can refinance for only $395, don't tell you that you may have a higher interest rate.

The last couple of observations as I try to make my point include those pesky online pop-ups for low mortgage rates in every state. They are also sent to hundreds of lenders who pay a high price for any leads that are generated.

The last little scheme that is becoming a hot topic on mortgage sites is the credit bureaus who sell your information to lenders after you apply to a lender for your loan, making you the target of every mortgage telemarketer on the planet, some good, some bad. So much for privacy. Your job is to weed out the hundreds of callers and find a legitimate lender.

So now you have TV, Internet, telemarketers and even the good old post office delivering one direct mail piece after another — all to get you to sign on with them for your mortgage.

As you read more remember the old saying, if it sounds too

good to be true, it probably is. Your best bet is to check with your Better Business Bureau, the local banking department, or even the Chamber of Commerce for history on the lender of your choice. Find out if any complaints have been filed and if so, how many. Another tip is to make at least four calls to find a lender. Check with friends and relatives who have had a good experience. These tips will help you make a better decision and more than likely will put you into that first home.

THE MESSAGE

Owning your first home is now a privilege rather than a right. This bold statement may not be what a first time homebuyer wants to hear, but rather than shower readers with the worn out clichés of achieving the American Dream, I would like to help you understand what is really happening in the world of mortgages and home buying. I would like to help ensure that you don't fall into the hands of those who prey on first time buyers or those programs that simply sound too good to be true.

My first recommendation is to do your homework. Find a reliable realtor in the community who is known for his work ethic and honesty versus how much he spends in advertising. Don't be afraid to ask the hard questions and don't be afraid to fire your realtor or mortgage consultant. This is the biggest decision you will make for the next three to five years. Once you have a trustworthy realtor, seek out a mortgage lender with the same qualities. Stay away from those who make it sound like it's too good to be true.

Now that you are armed with real professionals, begin your

search and understand what it means to afford your first home. Don't be disappointed when at first it seems that all homes are out of your range. Stay the course and keep the prices and payments in perspective with what you can afford.

Remember realtors and lenders are there to make money. This means you must look out for your best interests.

The first thing you will need to do is get a pre-approval letter. This is not a pre-qualification letter. The difference is that a pre-approval is an actual approval. A pre-qualification is simply a letter stating that you make enough income to cover all your debts plus a new mortgage payment with all the extras like taxes, insurance, and sometimes the dreaded private mortgage insurance (PMI). (Hint: never pay PMI!) A "pre-qual" letter is nothing more than an opinion with no credit report and no underwriting to back it up.

Before you talk with your lender about a pre-approval, do some homework of your own. As a first-time home buyer, you will find significant opportunities to get the best financing available. The first thing you should do is check with the local office of your state housing authority. They offer the best possible rates and programs. Tell your lender that these rates are what you would like to be pre-approved for. Allow the lender to determine if in fact you qualify for the program and move forward. In the event you do not qualify, begin the process with your lender of finding out what program works best for you.

I will caution you now about programs to be very careful about and also give you clues to watch for to determine whether your lender is really on your side. For many buyers there is a variety of programs which allow you to state that you make enough to cover all the debt involved. This is a "Stated Income" program. If your lender states that you should just say that you make enough money to cover the costs involved when you really do not, this is a clue that you should move onto another lender. This type of program could put you and your new home in serious jeopardy down the road.

Other programs to watch for may be the 100 percent program and the "No Income No Asset" type programs. These programs do fit individuals with certain employment backgrounds who can benefit. But these same programs can put unsuspecting house hunters and those with limited knowledge into bankruptcy or foreclosure. I caution every first-time buyer to recognize that while it is a wonderful feeling to have your own home, you must pay the mortgage. A very simple rule that lenders have is, "You pay, you stay. You don't, we take!"

So now, you have a reliable realtor who is showing you homes that fit your budget. You have a lender or mortgage broker whom you trust to steer you in the right direction. All that's left for you is to be sure that the program you choose and the price that you pay allow you enough wiggle room to stay in your new home and enjoy all it has to offer!

Sometimes buyers think they have died and gone to heaven only to find out that they have a mortgage that will increase suddenly to a level so high that the payment cannot be made. Or sometimes the buyer arrives at the closing table only to find out that the lender or broker he chose forgot to tell him that the closing costs would be double. Simple solution, you think—just don't close? That may sound like a reasonable way to correct the situation, except that you, the buyer, are now in violation of the contract!

Far fetched you say? Not really. The world of real estate and mortgage lending is filled with many ethical people dedicated to helping buyers obtain that first home. Then again, there are those, as in any business, who want only to see the check.

I've outlined for you a fairly simple approach to being successful and given you pitfalls that lie ahead of all buyers. Find solid individuals to help you understand as much as possible about the process and you too will have that new home.

Joe Adamaitis

Mr. Adamaitis has been the President and owner of Direct Mortgage Services, Inc., in Portsmouth, New Hampshire for the past five years and has offices in Connecticut and Florida. The company was recently purchased by Direct Capital Corporation, also located in Portsmouth. Mr. Adamaitis has been in the mortgage-banking world since 1979 and has been in all facets of the business. He is an active member of the New Hampshire Mortgage Bankers Association and the National Mortgage Brokers Association and is a frequent writer for many publications including RESPA.com. He participates with the legislative committee in his home state and focuses on issues to serve the borrowers. If you have questions you may e-mail him at joe@directmortgageservice.com

The advantages of home ownership can far outweigh the difficulties of buying a home or of maintaining it.

1

WHY BUY A HOUSE?

F acing high home prices and the attendant financial obligations of home ownership, many people today view a home purchase as well beyond their reach. The advantages of home ownership, however, can far outweigh the difficulties of buying a home or of maintaining it.

The most important advantage to most people is having a house of their own, but a house is first an investment and very likely the largest investment most people will ever make. If a home is properly maintained and local market conditions remain favorable, it will increase in value, a process referred to as appreciation. As the mortgage on the house is paid off, while home values rise, the owner's return-on-investment increases in value as well, a process referred to as gaining equity. Homeowners may borrow against their equity to finance home repairs or to consolidate other debts, but for most people, equity on their home is a nest egg and part of their retirement planning. Moreover, there are tax benefits stemming from home ownership allowing the deduction of home mortgage interest. Millions of happy homeowners can attest to the fact that owning your own home may be the best financial decision you could ever make.

To Rent or to Own

For most people the decision to buy a home is a comparison between renting an apartment or house and buying a house. The following real-life example, placed in Las Vegas, one of the fastest growing housing markets in the United States, is instructive.

After 14 years of renting at $9,000 a year a couple purchased their first home. During that time, the demand for housing in Las Vegas grew dramatically, so the purchase prices of both new and older homes went up. Had the couple purchased a home when prices were down, they could have acquired a nice property in a good neighborhood for nearly the same amount they had paid in rent over the 14 years.

Using an estimated sales price of $130,000 for the house, a fixed interest rate of 8 percent, a mortgage term of 30 years, and a down payment of 20 percent of the purchase price, consider the following comparison with other expenses included:

RENTING VS. OWNING A HOUSE		
	Renting	Owning
Monthly payment	$800.00	$763.12
Electricity	$ 50.00	$50.00
Gas	$14.00	$14.00
Water	$12.00	$12.00
Renters'/Hazard insurance [1]	$21.67	$27.08
Property taxes monthly [2]	N/A	$100.75
Total	$897.67	$966.95

[1] Annual premium divided by 12, renters' insurance might be less because it only protects furnishing and personal belongings within the rented property.

[2] Annual taxes divided by 12. Amount calculated based on local percentage applied to the sales price; every county in every state has a different percentage.

Though the financial advantages of owning a home seem nominal as viewed in this chart, it is important to remember that there are tax and other financial benefits stemming from home ownership as well.

Another way to explain how the couple could have paid almost half of their mortgage during the same 14-year period in which they were renting is with the help of an amortization table. This tool explains in detail how the monthly payment is allocated into principal, the actual amount of money borrowed, and interest, essentially the cost of using the bank's or mortgage company's money. Initially, the interest paid far outweighs the principal paid, but gradually the allocation reverses.

30-YEAR AMORTIZATION CHART			
Year	Interest	Principal	Balance
1	8,320.00	868.84	103,131.16
2	8,250.49	940.95	102,190.21
3	8,175.22	1,019.05	101,171.16
4	8,093.69	1,103.63	100,067.53
5	8,005.40	1,195.23	98,872.30
6	7,909.78	1,294.44	97,577.86
7	7,806.23	1,401.87	96,175.99
8	7,694.08	1,518.23	94,657.76
9	7,572.62	1,644.24	93,013.52
10	7,441.08	1,780.71	91,232.81
11	7,298.62	1,928.51	89,304.30
12	7,144.34	2,270.26	87,034.04
13	6,962.72	2,277.01	84,757.03
14	6,780.56	2,466.00	82,291.04
15	6,583.28	2,902.99	79,388.05
16	6,351.04	2,911.62	76,476.43
17	6,118.11	3,153.28	73,323.15
18	5,865.85	3,415.00	69,908.15
19	5,592.65	3,698.45	66,209.70
20	5,296.78	4,005.42	62,204.29
21	4,976.34	4,337.86	57,866.42
22	4,629.31	4,697.90	53,168.52
23	4,253.48	5,087.83	48,080.69
24	3,846.46	5,510.11	42,570.58
25	3,405.65	5,967.45	36,603.13
26	2,928.25	6,462.75	30,140.38
27	2,411.23	6,394.34	23,746.05
28	1,899.68	7,480.01	16,266.04
29	1,301.28	8,100.85	8,165.19
30		8,165.19	0.00
TOTAL	172,914.26	104,000.00	276,914.26

The table shows that in 14 years, 21 percent of the loan amount of $104,000 would have been paid. Moreover, while the difference in monthly payments for renting and owning a house, including other expenses, would have been only $69.28, the rise in home values in Las Vegas over those years would have increased the couple's wealth rather than depleting it as paying rent does by taking money without returning anything of value. If the property were assessed today, given the rapid growth in housing demand in the Las Vegas housing market, its value would very likely approach 300 percent of its original purchase value, almost $390,000, and the couple's equity would be approximately $286,000.

There are other matters to consider when buying a home, of course. Home ownership, as a financial investment, is long-term. If your career or personal situation forces you to move often, a home purchase may not be a good idea. The incidental costs of a home purchase, a slow housing market, the need for upgrades or restorations, and other considerations all weigh against purchasing a home if its owners will not reside in it for more than two years. Before you make the decision to buy a house, reevaluate your personal finances, how much you have saved, and whether you are financially prepared to maintain a home.

YOUR FINANCES

Before You Make a Decision

The savings rate in the United States has not been as low as it currently is since the days of the Great Depression. The reasons for that are complex, and while there are many long-term strategies for budgeting expenses to increase savings, they won't help you very much if want to buy a home now.

In subsequent chapters, methods for purchasing a home with no down payment and no closing costs will be discussed, as well as other ways of reducing the costs of buying a home, but lenders still need to know that you have financial reserves to cover unforeseen expenses, in addition to the normal fees and processing costs associated with a mortgage agreement. The lender will look closely at checking or savings accounts, financial instruments, personal or employer retirement plans, and other liquid assets, so it is very important that your financial affairs be in order before taking another step.

How Much Can You Afford?

If your financial affairs are in order, you may wish to be pre-qualified by a bank, credit union, or mortgage broker. A pre-qualification does not mean the lender has an obligation to fund your home purchase, but it does indicate how much you can afford and gives you leverage in the home buying process. Your financial history will be reviewed, and you will be asked to provide information such as your income, monthly credit payments, and credit balances and the type of debt.

On your own, you can calculate how much you can afford to borrow to purchase a home by using the worksheet on the following page.

PRLIMINARY CALCULATIONS ON HOUSE AFFORDABILITY		
	Monthy	**Notes**
GROSS INCOME		
Wages	$5,000	
Other		
TOTAL	$5,000	
DEBT		
Auto Loan	$350	
Credit Card	$50	
Credit Card	$100	
Student Loan	$75	
TOTAL	$575	
Principal & Interest	$1650	calculated with the debt-to-income ratio: 35 percent
Total estimated monthy payment	$1650	
Total monthly debt	$2,225	
Total DTI Ratio	**44.5 percent**	

"Gross income" refers to your monthly earnings before taxes. Enter minimum payments required for each credit account listed under "debt." Multiply your gross income by 35 percent. The result will be the approximate monthly payment you can afford, and it will be added to your other debt and divided by your total gross income to determine the debt-to-income ratio. The maximum DTI Ratio will be explained in Chapter 7, where current types of loans are discussed.

TAX ADVANTAGES OF HOME OWNERSHIP

As mentioned earlier, there are significant tax benefits associated with home ownership, and they are a commonly cited incentive for new buyers. The best reference explaining the provisions of the tax code pertaining to home ownership is IRS Publication 530, "Tax information for First-Time Homeowners," now available online.[3]

IRS 530 outlines certain rules regarding deductions for home mortgage interest:

- The home loan must be secured by a qualified home — a main home or principal place of residence — or a second home that might be a house, condo, trailer, boat, or similar property that has sleeping, cooking, and toilet facilities. A second home need not be rented out even if it is unoccupied by the owner during the year.

- A secured loan is one in which an instrument (such as mortgage, deed of trust, or land contract) pegs the payment of the debt to the property owner and provides, in case of default, that the house itself is the collateral for the loan. It is recorded under any state or local law that applies.

- In addition, the loan must be in the owner's name. Mortgage interest payments cannot be deducted when made on behalf of others if you are not legally responsible for making payments. Both the homeowner and the lender must intend that the loan be repaid. There must be a true debtor-creditor relationship between the individual claiming deductions and the lender.

[3] See Annex C.

Which Closing or Settlement Fees Are Deductible?

- **Prepaid interest.** A homeowner can deduct the interest paid at settlement if deductions are itemized, but this amount should be included in the mortgage interest statement provided by the lender that funded the loan.

- **Points and loan origination fees.** Generally, points, a percentage of the loan amount determined by the lender, are a settlement-cost paid to "buy down" the interest rate. (This option will be discussed in Chapter 7). The general rule dictates that the full amount of points cannot be deducted in the year paid because they are considered prepaid interest, so they must be deducted over the term of the mortgage. Any exception must meet all the following tests:

    - The house is the main place of residence and is the collateral for the loan.

    - Paying points is an established business practice in the area where the loan was originated.

    - The points paid were not more than the points generally charged in that area.

    - Income is reported in the year earned and expenses reported in the year incurred.

    - The points were not paid in place of amounts that ordinarily are stated separately on the settlement statement such as appraisal fees, inspection fees, title fees, attorney fees, and property taxes.

    - Paid along with the points was either a down

payment, earnest money deposit, or other funds, and they must have been out-of-pocket, not provided by the lender.

- The loan was used to build or buy a main home.

- The points were calculated as a percentage of the principal amount of the mortgage.

- The amount was clearly stated and shown in the settlement statement as points — charges for the mortgage.

The same rules apply to the loan origination fee.

- **Real estate taxes.** Property taxes can also be deducted. The presence of an escrow account, money held by the lender that is collected and dispersed periodically for tax and insurance payments (escrow accounts will be addressed in Chapter 8), cannot be deducted by monthly allotment but must be deducted according to the amounts the lender pays to the county assessor quarterly on the homeowner's behalf. Additionally, if property taxes are paid upfront at the time of closing because the seller's escrow accounts do not cover outstanding balances (a rare occurrence, thankfully), those payments must be claimed on an annual return.

Which Closing or Settlement Fees Are Not Deductible?

- Insurance, including fire and comprehensive coverage, as well as title and mortgage insurance (mortgage insurance protection, or MIP, is explained in Chapter 9).

- Appraisal fees.

- Notary fees.

- Costs of preparation and processing the mortgage note or deed of trust.

- Mortgage insurance premiums.

- VA funding fees.

These fees can be rolled into the cost of the home if the home is to be sold or the mortgage refinanced. Further information on these fees and costs is found in Chapter 8.

Is All the Interest That You Pay on Your Mortgage Fully Deductible?

Home mortgage interest may be deducted if the conditions listed in the first three paragraphs of this section are met. Additionally, the loan must be taken out to buy, build or improve a home (home acquisition debt) and the total debt is less than $1 million, and less than $500,000 if married but filing returns separately.

What Are Mortgage Interest Statements

If more than $600 in mortgage interest is paid during the year, the homeowner should receive an IRS Form 1098, or similar statement, issued by the lender no later than January 31 of the following year, showing total interest paid on a mortgage throughout the year. If a main home is purchased during the year, the statement will also show the deductible points paid and any points paid by the seller, which might also be deducted.

Keep in mind that the tax code changes from year to year and that a consultation with a tax advisor or accountant is recommended.

2

GETTING STARTED

I f, after weighing the advantages and disadvantages of purchasing your own home, you decide it's the right thing for you, you'll want to find the right people to help make the process go smoothly. Look for:

- A licensed real-estate professional.

- A mortgage broker or knowledgeable lender.

- An attorney, preferably specializing in real-estate law.

In this section, the focus is on finding the right home for you, understanding the role of the real-estate professional, and developing a budget that defines your search and prepares you for pre-closing and closing costs required to close the deal.

FINDING THE BEST REAL-ESTATE PROFESSIONAL FOR YOU

Many new home buyers believe it easier and less expensive to find their dream home by themselves and that, in any case, a real-estate agent only looks out for the seller's interests. However, a reputable real-estate agent must look out for buyers' interests to stay in business, and his or her experience with the process and the law can be invaluable to you.

Upon sale of the property, a real-estate broker or agent does earn a commission from the seller of between 3 percent and 7 percent of the home sales price. Normally, a buyer pays no additional fees to the listing agent. Any agent might show and negotiate a listed home whether that home is listed with him or not, but in that case, the seller's fee is generally split between the listing agent with whom the seller has a contract and the agent responsible for the sale. Some buyers choose to engage the services of a buyer's agent, a broker or agent who markets his or her services as advocating the interests of the buyer instead of the seller, and the buyer may have to pay additional fees to that agent.

Take time to research and understand the role of real estate professionals since they will be the persons working most closely with you throughout the home-buying process.

There are three qualifying types of real state professionals:

- **Real estate broker:** an individual who has passed a state qualifying exam and is thereby eligible to open a real estate office and receive earnings for real estate services.

- **Sales agent:** an entry-level real estate professional who has not yet passed a qualifying exam, thereby requiring a broker to sponsor him or her. A sales agent or salesperson works for the broker.

- **Realtor:** a real estate professional who is a member of the National Association of Realtors and has adopted the NAR code of ethics and practice standards. Realtors are generally full-time agents who have demonstrated commitment to being an expert in the real estate industry financially, educationally, and professionally.

Generally, you will enlist the services of an agent to assist you in your home search, but an agent will also help explain and avoid legal complexities, will explain the elements of the buying process and the necessary documentation, and will act as mediator in difficult negotiations.

It's prudent to consider several agents and to assess their level of reliability, experience, and professionalism. Agents with high annual sales volumes and with visible presence in the area in which you are looking are a good place to start, but also look for agents who might specialize in the types of properties you want — multiple-family dwellings, farms, upscale homes, limited deeds. If you have friends in the area, ask them who helped them buy their homes. Evaluate professionals' qualifications, including whether they are realtors. Meet with them, and ensure that you are comfortable, of like minds, and that they are approachable.

Things you might consider:

1. Do they have a callback policy? Do they have a cell phone number?

2. Are they full-time agents?

3. Do they consider themselves a buyer's agent, a seller's agent, or a dual agent (see below)? The answer may affect your decision to pay for the services of a buyer's agent.

4. Do they seem capable of negotiating for you? Will they aggressively research available options that suit your stated needs and desires?

5. What is their experience in the area? Are they knowledgeable about home prices, costs of living, schools, services, and the many other factors that might affect your decision to buy?

A real estate agent may represent clients in one of three ways:

- **As a seller's agent:** This is the listing agent, meaning the seller contracted the agent to list the property for sale and catalog the listing in the Multiple Listing Service (MLS). The listing agent earns the full commission if he or she sells the property but splits the commission with another agent if that agent is responsible for showing and selling the home. In that sense, even if the other agent is a buyer's agent, his or her earnings come largely from the seller.

- **As a buyer's agent:** A buyer's agent is committed through a written agreement to represent your interests throughout the buying and closing process. In some states the buyer's agent is allowed to charge a minimum fee for his services. As mentioned, he will also get a split of the commission from the seller's agent. Often, a buyer's agent will not charge for the services provided to you and will agree to receive a share of the commission on the house sale in payment for their services. Before signing an agreement with an agent to represent you, negotiate the agent's fees. Ensure the agreement includes a statement specifying the commission the agent will receive (commonly a percentage) and who is responsible for its payment[4]. Keep in mind that the agreement is negotiable.

- **As a dual agent:** An agent who declares that he or she will be working for both buyer and seller[5]. In theory, all buyers' agents are dual agents in that they receive at least a portion of their payment in the form of a commission derived from the seller's contract with the listing agent. In practice, however, dual agents will improve the seller's chances of selling the property at a fair-market price while negotiating on your behalf to ensure an agreeable price and a problem-free buying process.

Do not sign any agreement or provide personal financial information or the amount you are willing to spend for a house until you have chosen a real estate professional. After you make your decision, your agent will need that information and more to assist you effectively. Your agent will have to know whether you are pre-qualified and for how much, if your credit history or financial situation present potential problems that might affect the loan process or alter the choice of home you can afford, and the specifications of the property you desire.

Keep in mind that even though you may be pre-qualified for a certain loan amount, buying an expensive house may not

[4]See annex B for a sample on a buyer's agent agreement.
[5]See annex B for a sample on a dual agent's disclosure.

be prudent, especially if you are buying a house for the first time. Let your agent know if you're willing to put sweat equity into a less expensive older home by making upgrades and improvements as you build financial equity and improve your financial situation. These strategies will be discussed in greater detail later.

Most importantly, it is essential that you choose an agent you trust, work with him or her, and always let your agent know if you see or hear about a home that seems to fit your requirements.

THE BUDGET

There are many things to consider when buying a house for the first time, but perhaps most important is your ability to pay a mortgage and whether you will have enough for a down-payment, pre-closing, and closing costs.

In Chapter 1, you had the opportunity to calculate a rough estimate of a monthly payment you could afford, but acquiring the property may require a down payment and closing costs paid up front.

For example, if the house you have chosen is priced at $175,000, you will need:

DOWN PAYMENT	CLOSING COSTS
3 percent = 175,000 x .03 equals $5,250 10 percent = 175,000 x .10 equals $17,500 15 percent = 175,000 x .15 equals $26,250 20 percent = 175,000 x .20 equals $35,000	These are additional settlement fees that you would have to pay to the lender, mortgage broker, attorney, escrow and title companies, the county recorder and the appraiser. They could be between two to seven percent of the house sales price. Closing costs will be explained in more detail in Chapter 8.

The Down Payment

To understand fully the way down payments are calculated, it's first necessary to list and explain the different types of loans available. You may or may not qualify for all of them.

- **Conventional conforming and nonconforming loans:** For these types of loans, probably the most common, lenders usually ask for a 20 percent down payment on the house sales price. If the loan-to-value ratio is more than 80 percent you will have to pay the lender Private Mortgage Insurance (PMI) which is normally 0.75 percent of the loan amount and insures the lender against your default of the loan.

- **Federal Housing Administration (FHA) loans:** These are government secured loans available to qualifying individuals. They were instituted to provide financing options to lower-income citizens. The down payment you will have to pay on a FHA loan is 3 percent of the sales price as minimum.

- **Veterans Administration (VA) loans:** Veterans may qualify for a VA guaranteed loan with 100 percent financing on the purchase of their home and no down payment.

The Closing Costs

Closing costs vary, but you do have options in arranging for their payment:

- **Gifts**. You may suggest that donations toward these costs be gifts or wedding presents.

- **Concessions**. These normally come from the seller or builder. Because the closing costs are included in the purchase price, you may have to pay more for the house, but that may be preferable to depleting your savings or having insufficient funds to cover the costs.

- **Lenders' special programs**. Some lenders are willing to "roll over" the closing costs into the total loan amount. The loan amount will be from 103-105 percent of the original loan amount and points or interest rates may increase.

- **Housing assistance programs**. If you meet moderate-income guidelines, you may be eligible for state or local loans or even grants because you are a first-time home buyer. More information is provided in Chapter 5.

- **Employer assistance.** Some big companies have housing-assistance programs available for its employees.

- **Retirement plans.** You can take a loan out against your retirement account (IRA, 401(k), life insurance, or other controlled type savings. See Chapter 7.

HOW TO CHOOSE THE HOUSE THAT BEST SUITS YOU

There are many things to consider when buying a home, and most have a bearing on the quality of your life there. Crime rates, school ratings, proximity to stores and services, your jobs, and many more aspects of living in your new home will be of importance to you, but when purchasing a home, your primary consideration has to be its value as an investment — what will be its worth when it comes time to sell.

In the world of real estate, there are only three rules: location, location, and location. That's an old joke, but if your neighborhood declines, schools are poor, taxes are high, or any of a dozen other factors cause the value of your home to depreciate rather than appreciate over time, you won't be laughing.

Part of what makes a good choice for you depends on the pros and cons of the different types of real estate property like new houses, manufactured houses, condos, town houses, gated communities, and resale houses.

How to Find the Right Neighborhood

Every search needs a place to begin. If you are renting a house or apartment in a neighborhood you like, that's a good place to begin your search. Most people, though, want to improve on their living situation, not simply buy a home. For them, and possibly you, there are important things to consider:

- **Is the neighborhood safe?** Your real state agent can provide statistical information on crime rates for any neighborhood or area. Gated communities, or developments with controlled access, usually provide additional security, though that usually increases the price of the property and the cost of living there, to say nothing of restrictive rules for residents.

If you are seriously considering a home, arrange to visit with residents of the area and ask them about any safety concerns that have become an issue with people living in the area.

- **Is the neighborhood well maintained?** Neighborhoods in which many of the homes are rental properties are often poorly maintained either by absentee landlords or uncaring renters. Sadly, better homes in such areas, while well-maintained, may be effectively overpriced because their value is dragged downwards over time by the surrounding properties. Purchasing such a home will mean you will never, as they say, see your money again.

- **Are the schools well-rated?** If you have children or plan to start a family, the importance of good schools is obvious, but whether you have a family or are single, the quality of neighborhood schools affects the value of your home and makes it more or less attractive to potential buyers when time to sell.

- **Is transportation accessible?** In urban areas, public transportation is often essential, and you will want to choose a home serviced by buses or trains. If you commute by car, you'll want well maintained and safe roads on which to travel and close proximity to stores, hospitals, and other services.

- **Is the economy of the area stable?** The economic

growth and stability of the area surrounding a home can influence its future property value. Essentially, that is an effect of supply and demand. As an economy improves, more people are able to purchase their own home. As long as the supply of new and older homes remains even with that increased demand for homes, the prices will remain stable. If too many homes are built or too few, the prices will fall or rise respectively. Obviously, your choice of home should be in an area experiencing economic growth, or at the very least, stability.

- **Leisure facilities and amenities.** Home buyers increasingly seek homes that are close to recreational facilities and other life-style amenities, particularly those who are buying homes for retirement or who are empty-nesters. The demand for homes in areas that feature such conveniences greatly increases the value of the properties, sometimes beyond the home's expected price.

There are also some important things to avoid when choosing a new home:

- Pass up houses that are next to factories, warehouses, or industrial corridors, even if its very cheap.

- Avoid homes near funeral homes for obvious reasons, but also avoid locations near churches and other institutions that might create parking problems and excessive foot traffic.

- Avoid locations near airports or under incoming and outgoing flight paths.

- Avoid properties that include or are part of a flood plain.

Often such areas are zoned as such and will result in higher insurance costs.

- Avoid streets with heavy traffic and intersections that are unsafe for children and the elderly.

TYPES OF PROPERTIES IN THE REAL ESTATE MARKET

Detached Houses

A detached home is a structure that shares no walls or systems with other structures and is freestanding on property delineated in a separate deed of ownership. When buying a detached house, you are buying both the structure and the rights to the land, which also means you have full liability and are fully responsible for maintenance and upkeep of both the structure and the land. That also means you have the greatest latitude in upgrading or renovating the home, a principal reason many people choose detached homes.

Things to Consider When Choosing a New House

Unless the house is a custom design, a new house is often what is called a tract house, one housing unit within a larger housing development. Usually constructed by a large building company, a tract house incorporates a design similar to other houses in the development, keeping design costs down. Differences from one tract house to another are usually minor exterior embellishments and interior upgrades chosen by the owner, all of which may affect the price of the home.

Unless the market has changed dramatically since the

beginning of the development project, it is unlikely you can negotiate the base price of a tract home. You can, however, negotiate upgrades.

Remember that housing developments take advantage of zoning for concentrated land use and that developers show greater profits by building many homes in an area serviced by the same septic, utility, and transportation systems. Zoning laws often allow structures to be built quite close together, so your chosen home may stand very close to that of your neighbor's, and you may have very little lawn space and even less privacy.

However, buying a new house has distinct advantages because you have a warranty from the builder on things like the air conditioning and heating system, plumbing, electrical installation, and the roof. In addition, new homes are not built using toxic materials such as lead paint and asbestos, among others, a persistent, expensive problem in older homes.

Also, financial incentives are often a part of the buying process for new homes. Builders routinely offer buyers incentives like paying the entire amount of the closing costs if the buyer closes the deal within a time specified by the builder, normally a month.

A word of caution: unfinished homes in uncompleted developments are a strong indication that the buildings are pre-sales — construction is begun on the basis of a deposit — and that the builder may be underfinanced. Should the builder founder financially, the development may never be completed, and the value of your own home will drop precipitously. Investigate the financial strength of the builder when considering a tract home.

Things to Consider When Choosing a Resale House

A resale house is a property owned previously.

Older homes are often difficult and expensive to maintain, especially if they are more than 20 years old. Electrical systems might have to be brought up to local building codes, the air conditioning and heating system may have to be replaced, and the hot water tank, some plumbing and fixtures, and the roof will likely need to be replaced if the house is older than 15 years. Wet basements and attendant problems like mildew are common in older homes, and damage from termites or other pests is often difficult to detect but will surely make itself known eventually. Before purchasing the home, you should have it inspected. Home inspections, as part of the buying process, are explained later in more detail.

Older homes have had previous owners who may have had financial or legal problems that were left unresolved and have a bearing on the ownership of the house. There could be liens against the property that have to be satisfied to clear the title to the house. If the current owner refuses to resolve those issues, you may have to pay the liens to acquire the property. A title search, part of the home-buying process, is an investigation of the history of the title to the house and will reveal such situations.

A resale house is often less expensive than a new house, depending on location, condition, upgrades, and tax structure, and because the landscaping is already done, considerable savings can be realized financially and in time and effort.

Things to Consider When Choosing a Gated Community

Whether living in a new house or a resale house, home owners in gated communities are members of a home owners' association that charges a monthly fee and dictates certain rules regarding care and maintenance of the home, as well as bylaws concerning such things as parking, displays, noise, and other aspects of living in the community. There are many advantages to living in a gated community, despite its restrictions, not the least of which is added security due to the community's controlled access and the greater likelihood of appreciation of property values due to the emphasis on consistent maintenance and care.

Things to Consider When Choosing an Attached House

This classification is commonly thought of as communal living, meaning that while you own everything within the walls of your unit, you also share walls with adjoining units and share ownership of the land and other facilities. Often called villas, condos, or townhouses, attached homes usually include access to amenities such as a pool, playgrounds, gyms, spas, and other shared facilities, and require the payment of a monthly fee covering maintenance of the outside of your unit, the lawns and landscaping, and care of shared facilities. There are two types of attached residences:

- **A condominium.** Essentially apartments in either low-rise or high-rise buildings, condos are usually less expensive to purchase, are free of exterior and some interior maintenance costs, and offer much of the same security as a gated community. Like any apartment, though, convenience comes at the expense of privacy, and appreciation on the home's value is likely to be far less than that on a detached home.

- **A town house.** Usually, town houses are two-story residences in which the bedrooms are located upstairs. Often, they are in a gated community managed by a homeowners association, and the owner possesses the land on which the unit stands if it is situated in a planned unit development.

Manufactured Homes

Manufactured houses are an increasingly popular choice for many first-time home buyers, though they are considered personal property, not real estate, until they are placed on a permanent foundation A manufactured house, as the name implies, is produced in sections in a factory, and shipped to the home site. Because the unit arrives with nearly every component installed and is considerably less expensive than a home built onsite, many people choose manufactured homes as a beginner home or for retirement.

Manufactured homes are often found in communities designed especially for them where the owners lease the lots on which the home is placed and share community buildings, recreational facilities, and services like laundromats.

While cost and convenience are distinct advantages of manufactured homes, mortgage options are more limited, particularly if the home is not installed on a fixed foundation. Partly, the limited choices for mortgage loans is due to the fact that manufactured homes do not appreciate as conventional homes do and, in fact, usually depreciate in value. Lenders are reluctant to give mortgage loans on properties whose value does not outlast the term of the mortgage.

Bargains and Fixer-Uppers

Properties whose owners can no longer make the payments on the mortgage go to foreclosure and are repossessed either by the lender, HUD, or Fannie Mae (Federal National Mortgage Association). These foreclosed properties are subsequently offered for sale to the general public at prices lower than their market price because the entities that repossessed them want to get their money back as soon as they can. Foreclosed homes are listed in the MLS as any other home, and the buying process is exactly the same as when buying a house directly from an individual or builder with the exception — and it is a big exception — that they are sold "as is." While some are acceptable dwellings, many will require an investment of capital or sweat equity to make them livable.

A second option is to find a fixer-upper, a house sold "as is" and usually requiring extensive renovations to both the exterior and the interior. They are often on the market because the owners are unwilling or unable to invest the money and time to improve the properties. Handy home buyers should expect the worst, but the advantage of a fixer-upper is that costs can be controlled, the quality of renovations can be better overseen, and much of the labor can be done by the owners themselves.

*You've found
your dream home!
Now what?*

3

YOU HAVE FOUND
YOUR DREAM HOME

At this point, let's assume you and your agent have located the home of your dreams. It's in a nice neighborhood, appears affordable, seems in reasonable condition, and fits your lifestyle to a tee. You determined your budget, got your financial affairs in order, did your research on locations and types of homes, made a list of the criteria that would meet your budget and your lifestyle, and employed the use of very knowledgeable professionals—all good, but what now?

SHOULD YOU HIRE AN ATTORNEY?

The answer to this question largely depends on the location of the property you wish to purchase. In some eastern states, an attorney is in charge of handling all the legalities involved in a purchase including the review of various contracts, resolving irregularities in the title or land survey, and explaining agreements signed at closing, including arrangements for tax and insurance escrow accounts. On the other hand, in many west coast states, escrow and title companies are in charge of the escrow and closing process and the services of an attorney are rarely required.

Still, you may want to retain the services of a real estate law expert in the event you encounter legal difficulties during the buying process or simply want a legal expert to review the contracts and other legal documents commonly required during the purchase process.

Problems do sometimes arise. A young woman moving to Las Vegas was recently forced to hire a real estate attorney to file a lawsuit because a selling agent accepted a second offer on the property she had chosen after he accepted her offer. The lawsuit laid claim to the purchase rights on the property. Facing the lawsuit, the seller agreed to compensate the woman financially.

It is also not uncommon for owners to sell their property themselves. With no sales agent involved in the transactions, you are left with no one to advise you on the legal process of buying a home. In that case hiring an attorney would be prudent.

If you do decide to retain the legal services of an attorney, be very careful to choose a lawyer who specializes in real estate law. Inquire at the local bar association or call the state board of real estate agents for more information about real estate legal professionals in your area.

MAKING THE BEST OFFER

Your next step is to make a formal offer on the house. When your agent sends the offer to the listing agent, three things can happen: the seller accepts your offer; the seller rejects your offer—the search begins again; or the seller returns a counteroffer—negotiations begin.

How to Calculate Your Offer

The best way to know what to offer is to research the values of comparable houses that were sold in the same neighborhood during the previous four months, or if none were sold, the values of comparable homes currently on the market. Your agent will have access to all this information, including recent assessments, but insist on a meeting to discuss your agent's sources, evaluations, and conclusions and whether the other homes used as a basis for your offer are comparable to the home you've chosen.

Have ready your pre-qualification paperwork so the seller will know that you will likely be approved for the loan amounts that support your bid, a fact that might affect his choice among potential buyers.

The Negotiation

For the most part, your agent will act as the go-between in negotiations with the seller, but final decisions are always yours, so you should be aware of how things are done.

- The seller should be made aware of the basis for your offer. Statistical information and comparable home values should be compiled for presentation, if necessary.

- Put a limit on the price you are willing to pay even if the seller can justify a higher asking price, but be prepared to be flexible when negotiating on individual elements of the deal.

- Do not let anyone know how much you want the property; this could be used against you by the listing agent.

- If you increase your bid, look for something in exchange. Home protection plans and warranties covering any defects on resale houses are very cost-effective inducements for sellers that might also relieve them of liability if serious problems arise following the sale or if conditions they declared during the sale prove false. Sellers commonly assume a portion of the closing costs, as well.

- Stick with your plan and keep to your budget. Do not be influenced by sales pressure that could raise the price unnecessarily, such as the seller's agent suggesting there is a better offer than yours that could be beaten if your offer were higher.

The Purchase Agreement

The purchase agreement or contract is the most important document in the process of acquiring a house. Included on the contract are:

- Your name and current address.

- The seller's name.

- The names of the agents representing you and the seller.

- The property description and its furnishings.

- The estimated close of the deal (close of escrow).

- The amount of the good faith deposit, commonly known as the earnest money deposit, a concept explained later in this chapter.

- Which closing costs will be paid by whom (buyer and/or seller).

- The escrow and title company names, among others.

This contract must be fully executed (signed by all parties) to proceed with the financing of the house. Your agent is responsible for getting all necessary information from the listing agent.

It is very important that you read every single line of the contract; don't feel hurried. Do not sign a purchase contract that has blank spaces. The only thing not known at that moment is the interest rate of your loan; the agent will leave that space blank. Your agent or the seller's agent should write "N/A" in the spaces that don't apply to that particular deal.

Keep in mind that by signing a purchase agreement, you are committing yourself to buy that property through a legal instrument, and should you change your mind, you can lose your earnest money deposit unless the situation causing you to retract your bid is out of your control.

Earnest Money Deposit

An earnest money deposit (EMD) is a good faith deposit that the escrow company or attorney receives for deposit in an escrow account to assure the seller that your bid is sincere and you are committed to the deal. The amount of EMD is usually stated within the purchase agreement.

INSPECTIONS

Before ordering a home inspection made by a professional licensed inspector (this applies to resale properties), inspect the property yourself looking for any problems or issues that may be revealed by the inspector. Minor decorating details are not subject to the checklist inspection, but anything seeming out of the ordinary should be brought to the inspector's attention.

The property must be inspected by a licensed residential inspector who will provide a checklist that will help you understand the scope and focus of the inspection. The home inspection is recommended by real estate professionals because it can help to determine potential and existing problems with the property that may affect your decision to buy, but more likely will affect the price, work that must be done before the sale, and hazards that must be abated before you occupy the home.

The inspection fee is assumed by the buyer and ranges from $150 to $350.

Licensed inspectors are governed by the standards of practice of the American Society of Home Inspectors, and based on those standards they have to review and provide you with all the information regarding the condition of the house as follows:

Structural System

- The foundation and framing, the floor, walls, ceiling and roof structures.

Exterior

- Exterior wall covering, flashing, and trim.

- All exterior doors.

- Attached decks, balconies, stoops, steps, porches, and their associated railings.

- The eaves, soffits, and fascias.

- The vegetation, grading, surface drainage, and retaining walls on the property when any of these are likely to affect the building.

- Walkways, patios, and driveways leading to the house entrances.

Roof System

- The roof covering.

- The roof drainage systems.

- The flashings.

- The skylights, chimneys, and roof penetrations.

Plumbing System

- The interior water supply and distribution systems, including all fixtures and faucets.

- The drain, waste, and vent systems, including all fixtures.

- The water heating equipment.

- The vent systems, flues, and chimneys.

- The fuel storage and fuel distribution systems.

- The drainage sumps, sump pumps, and related piping.

- The inspector has to determine whether water supply and waste disposal systems are public or private and the quantity and quality of the water supply.

Electrical System

- The service drop.

- Service entrance conductors, cables, and raceways.

- Service equipment and main disconnects.

- Service grounding.

- Interior components of service panels and sub-panels.

- Conductors.

- Over-current protection devices.

- A representative number of installed lighting fixtures, switches, and receptacles.

- The ground fault circuit interrupters.

- The inspector has to describe the amperage and voltage rating of the service.

- The location of mains, disconnects, and sub panels.

- The wiring methods.

- The absence of smoke detectors.

Heating System

- The installed heating equipment.

- The vent systems, flues, and chimneys.

- The energy source.

- The heat supply adequacy or distribution balance must be determined.

Air Conditioning Systems

- The installed central and through-wall cooling equipment.

- The energy source.

- The cooling method by its distinguishing characteristics.

- Cooling supply adequacy or distribution balance.

Interior

- The walls, ceilings, and floors.

- Steps, stairways, and railings.

- The countertops and a representative number of installed cabinets.

- A representative number of doors and windows.

- Garage doors and garage door operators.

Insulation and Ventilation

- The insulation and vapor retarders in unfinished spaces.

- The ventilation of attics and foundation areas.

- The mechanical ventilation systems.

Fireplaces and Solid Fuel Burning Appliances

- The system components.

- The vents systems, flues, and chimneys.

- Fireplaces and solid burning appliances must be described.

- Draft characteristics.

- Fireplace inserts or stoves or firebox contents must be moved for inspection.

Some interior characteristics that the inspector will not review are:

- Paint, wallpaper, and other finished treatments.

- The carpeting.

- The window treatments.

- The central vacuum systems.

- The household appliances.

- Recreational facilities.

Though these items may be subject to negotiation on other grounds, the inspection itself does not comment on their condition.

Once you've done a pre-inspection walk-through and reviewed the items that will be included in the inspection report, plan to accompany the inspector to point out any irregularities you have observed yourself and to clarify any questions you might have regarding the condition of the house.

In some states, regulations regarding home inspections prior to sale are insufficient or lacking. In those cases, a home inspection is merely informative, but whether the inspection is governed by state or local laws or not, inspectors who are members of the American Society of Home Inspectors must follow the Society's Standards of Practice.

Following is a list of states having home inspection regulation laws[8] (States without qualifications listed require licensure):

- Alabama

- Alaska

- Arizona – Certification

- Arkansas – Registration

- California – Trade practice act

- Connecticut

- Georgia – Trade practice act

- Illinois

- Indiana

- Kentucky

- Louisiana

- Maryland

- Massachusetts

- Mississippi

- Montana – Trade practice act

- Nevada – Certification

- New Jersey

[8]Information provided by the American Society of Home Inspectors; www.ashi.org

- New York

- North Carolina

- Oklahoma

- Oregon – Certification

- Pennsylvania

- Rhode Island

- South Carolina

- South Dakota

- Tennessee

- Texas

- Virginia – Certification

- Wisconsin

Getting a Good Home Inspector

Most of the time, your real estate agent will recommend a specific home inspector to perform the inspection. Very often, the agent has a long-standing relationship with the inspector, and the recommendation is a good one. Nevertheless, the stakes are high and you should not hesitate to ask for the inspector's credentials and experience inspecting the particular type of property you are buying. If you are uncomfortable with the agent's recommendation, check the state licensee database (if your state has one) which may also list any complaints filed against a particular home inspector. You can also check the

American Society of Home Inspectors database.

The Inspection Process

Once you have decided whose services to retain, the inspection process is very easy. You will be provided with an inspection agreement,[9] normally before the inspection starts. If you've chosen to be present, be prepared to crawl under the house, climb into the attic, and onto the roof. After the inspection is complete, the inspector will provide you and the seller (through his or her agent) the final report on the house inspection. This could be a computer list report, a fill-in standardized report, or a report in the agent's own words explaining in detail the scope of the inspection and the results (this can be very helpful as long as it is comprehensive).

Negotiating After the Inspection

Essentially, an inspection ensures that you are not buying, a lemon, but every house has problems, and the inspection reveals those issues that may be the basis for further negotiations. If the problems will involve costly repairs or renovations, you certainly have leverage against the seller that can be used to negotiate a better deal.

What are some of the problems that might be of concern?

Exterior

- Patched concrete in driveways/service walks.

- Improperly pitched patios (this is a source of wet basements).

- Negative grading (this keeps water from moving away

[9]See appendix C for example of Inspection Agreement.

from the foundation walls).

- Roof with inadequate ventilation or soft spots.

- Roof covering curling, cracking, missing tabs/shingles/ tiles moss buildup, nail popping, or burn spots.

- Lack of gutters (extremely important element in basement dampness control).

- Wood siding that is in contact with the ground.

- Problems with the exterior electrical service, such as exposed wires.

- Garage door opener that does not work or does not have the safety reverse feature.

Interior

- Leaking pipes or faucets in kitchen, bathrooms or laundry room.

- Inadequate drainage.

- Poor water pressure.

- Moisture stains in wall and ceilings.

- Sloping floor or with penetrations.

- Rotted floors in bathrooms.

- Fireplace with open joints or cracks.

- Stairs in poor condition and with uneven risers.

- Structural problems observed from the attic.

Basement

- Foundation walls with cracks, leaks, or apparent movement.

- Moisture around drainage.

- Stained or rusted girders or columns.

- Rotted floor.

Plumbing

- Corroded and leaking pipes.

- Poor water pressure.

Heating System

- Gas-fired hot air units that are close to or beyond their normal life-expectancies (15-25 years) may become a source of carbon monoxide in the house.

- It may be a problem if the system was turned on using the thermostat and it did not start.

Cooling System

- Compressor or pump worn out.

- Cooling liquid.

- Vents do not open properly.

- Not right size unit for the house size.

Electrical – Main Panel

- Branch wires under sized — this is a safety hazard that can cause overheating and fire.

- System is not grounded.

- If the house is old (before late 70s) the Ground Fault Circuit Interrupts (G.F.C.I.) may be absent; you may have to upgrade part of the electrical system to avoid safety hazards.

If these or other problems are detected in the house, depending on the severity of the problem you might wish to hire a specialist to provide estimates on the costs of repair or renovation and the time it will take to make repairs. With that information in hand, you have three main options:

1. Negotiate for the seller to assume responsibility for the repairs through a contract addendum. If the repairs are major, you may have to wait longer to occupy the home.

2. Re-negotiate a lower price with the seller which takes into account the cost to you for repairs following the closing, and sign an "as is" addendum stating that you agree to receive the house in its current condition and are aware of the repairs or replacements needed. This option requires you to have the funds to make the repairs but allows you to control the costs and quality of work, have the work done while occupying the dwelling, and even to do some of the work yourself.

3. Back out of the deal and resume your search. You may lose your EMD, but that is better than putting good money after bad and depleting your savings and

endangering your financial security. Be sure that the purchase agreement you sign has the option to cancel the agreement based on findings of an inspection report. At the time of cancellation, you will have to provide the seller with a copy of the report containing the name, address, and telephone number of the inspector.

AGREEMENT ADDENDUMS AND THE COUNTEROFFER

Agreement Addendums

These are additions or changes to the original fully executed purchase agreement, which is to say it is signed by all parties (seller, buyer, and their respective agents) after the negotiations and settlement on the deal; addenda supersede the purchase agreement only in the specific clause(s) that their content addresses. Additions or changes to the purchase agreement could include but are not limited to:

- The original sales price.

- Who pays for the closing costs or what percentage is paid by the respective parties to the agreement.

- Who pays for the home appraisal fees and when.

- The addition or deletion of co-buyers.

- Revisions, additions, or deletions of repair costs assumed by the seller or accepted by the buyer following discovery during the inspection.

- Extension for the close of escrow.

Counteroffer

Documents supporting any counteroffer are used to further negotiations on the selling price, condition of the home and the assignment of responsibility for repairs, close of escrow, and many other topics. Your real estate agent will review and process all of them, but it is always your responsibility to read all the paragraphs in detail. Never feel hurried or hesitate to ask questions if you do not fully understand any element of a counteroffer or how the counteroffer affects the process.

THE APPRAISAL

An appraisal is submitted to your lender to confirm that the price you are paying for the house is fair. This is the first step following submission of your loan application. The loan processor or originator will order the appraisal and process the appraiser's report. This will be explained in more detail in Chapter 7.

CLASSIFIED CASE STUDIES
TM
directly from the experts

Real estate agents can provide the experience and knowledge of the marketplace to first-time homebuyers. Purchasing a home is a step-by-step process, and it's best for homebuyers to use experienced, full time agents. I have been a Realtor for 18 years, after having spent ten years as a teacher. I felt that I had all of the qualities that would make me a good professional.

To start, I meet all of my customers at my office, and we sit down for about 45 minutes, so I can explain in detail the home purchase process. Generally, I do not have a client-buyer relationship written agreement. However, approximately 25 percent of the time a client requests such an agreement to which I, of course, agree. I have even negotiated for the seller to pay the buyers' closing costs. I don't like to, but sometimes the financing that buyers are getting depends on it.

I absolutely encourage first-time homebuyers to get pre-qualified before searching for a home, so they are looking at homes they can comfortably afford. Most first-time buyers are looking for a freestanding, single family home. They are often coming out of apartments and want privacy and quiet. The average market value of a home in my area is $167,000.

Unfortunately, the first mistake many first-time homebuyers make is not pursuing mortgage options, which often include free down payment money from city coalitions that help them get into a home.

However, I have a lot of first-time homebuyer stories with happy endings. For example,

I had a buyer who had a limited income and two large dogs. I found a new listing on tour one morning and knew it would be gone before the day was out. It was perfect for this buyer.

The buyer worked nights and slept days. I went to his apartment and rang and knocked on the door until he groggily appeared. I made him jump into my car and see the house even though he was half asleep. He loved the home, and as we were leaving, I received a call from the listing agent who informed me she already had an offer coming in. I drove him right to the bank, got his mother to come, in case we needed a cosigner and wrote the offer for $500 more than any other offer that might come in. We got the house, and I even got him $5000 first-time homebuyer's assistance! He and his dogs were very pleased!

Ann Bailen
309-275-8181
309-661-7080
abailen@mindspring.com
www.annbailen.com

A native of Bloomington, Normal, Ann Bailen is a top producer with 18 years of experience in the real estate industry. She holds the professional designations of GRI and ABR and has a masters degree from the University of North Carolina.

*Building your
own home is a
challenge, and
if you're a first-
time buyer,
especially so.*

4

BUILDING YOUR OWN HOUSE

B uilding your own home is a challenge, and if you're a first-time buyer, especially so. You will have to plan and oversee a custom design, acquisition of the land, and construction of the building, and you will have to hire professional architects, real estate professionals, legal experts, and contractors to get the job done. Your financial planning will be far more complex, and you will have to plan with the unexpected in mind. The effort can be mind-boggling, but there are advantages to building your own home that far outweigh the difficulties.

PROS AND CONS

Pros

- You can choose to be your own general contractor, retaining control over materials and quality as well as cost.

- Financing is easier than purchasing a home if you already have free title on the land.

- You have more latitude in how to use your available funds and whether to allocate them for land or construction.

- Financing for land and construction can be consolidated.[10] (See more details in Chapter 7.)

- The house is custom-built to your specifications.

- Equity builds faster if the mortgage is based only on the construction or the land.

Cons

- You may have difficulties finding a builder if you decide to act as your own general contractor.

- The effort is very time consuming and will require you to deal with many people involving your constant attention and willingness to learn.

- Difficulties regarding missed deadlines and late or no payments are common when working with contractors or subcontractors

[10]Per Fannie Mae – Homestyle Construction to Permanent Mortgage

- You will have to keep exact records of expenditures to stay within budget and to produce documentation for tax purposes.

- If your loan is for the construction only, the lender might have guidelines regarding disbursements based on inspections and depending on how much of the job is done in a specific period previously established by the lender.

FINDING FINANCING

Lenders may be reluctant to offer loans to homebuyers who want to build a home. As you will soon see, building your own home is a complex process requiring you and the lender to be deeply involved for an extended period of time, and the risks to both of you are considerably greater than in a simple home resale or purchase.

The structure of the loans and the loan process are also different. When building your own home, you must first secure a construction loan to cover the building costs, then a permanent mortgage equal to the actual construction costs to pay off the construction loan and finance your ownership of the property. Moreover, disbursements of the construction loan are structured so that disbursements are incremental depending on the completion of defined phases of the construction process.

Finding financing for this kind of loan is possible through certain wholesale lenders and banks that offer such products. In this case, it would be better for you to work with a mortgage broker who will shop around to find a lender offering the program that best suits your financing requirements.

Some lenders offer combined financing for the construction and the land. Fannie Mae regulates a program called "The Homestyle Construction to Permanent Mortgage" that combines financing for the purchase of land, the construction of a new home, and a permanent mortgage into one loan with one closing, so that you may be able to lock the interest rate for the full term of the permanent mortgage before the actual construction begins. Other features of the program include borrowing up to 95 percent of the land purchase and cost of constructing the home, and paying closing costs for the full amount of the combined loan in a single payment.

Some wholesale lenders offer loans for the land with an "interest only" option over a one-year term, meaning payments are for interest only over that period and construction funds will only be disbursed after the one-year period. Advantages include building up savings for start-up costs and a contingency fund while developing plans and making other arrangements for construction.

HIRING A CONTRACTOR AND HOW MUCH IT COSTS

Where to Find a Residential General Contractor

Residential contractors are regulated by most state laws and must be licensed and bonded. Contractors must pass an extensive examination depending of their area of expertise; a contractor may have licenses to provide plumbing, electrical, or other construction services in addition to the general building license. Background investigations are also done to reveal any liens or lawsuits against them, convictions of any misdemeanors or felonies, bankruptcy proceedings, and other issues that might indicate they are a poor choice. Normally, contractors are regulated through a State Contractors Board, but if the state where you live does not require a contractor to be licensed, you will have to rely on word-of-mouth, the local Safety and Building Department, or the local Department of Consumer Affairs.

State Contractors Boards have licensee databases listing licensed contractors and pertinent information regarding their business backgrounds. The states where a licensure for contractors is required are starred below:

Source: ASAonline.com[11]

Other sources you might want to consider are construction associations which self-regulate their profession and which require their members to follow their standards of ethics and practice.

- The Associated General Contractors of America (**www.agc.org**)

- American Institute of Constructors (**www.aicnet.org**)

- American Subcontractors Association (**www.asaonline.com**)

- The National Association of Women in Construction (**www.nawic.org**)

- The Blue Book of Building and Construction (**www.thebluebook.com**)

Once you've compiled a list of contractors you feel will provide reliable services and are financially stable, you should:

- Get the contractors' full business information and personal contact information; ask for references (contact them), proof of licenses, insurance coverages, and bonding.

- Get detailed estimates from each contractor who passes your preliminary check.

- Check if there are any existing or past complaints at the Better Business Bureau (**www.bbbonline.org**).

- Retain a lawyer and discuss, in particular, state laws

pertaining to liens.

- Visit the site of the contractor's current project.

- Visit his place of business.

What Kind of Contractor to Hire

- **A General Contractor** is in charge of supervising big construction and remodeling jobs and usually oversees subcontractors who provide specialized services. The local Safety and Building Department can assist you regarding permits, plans, and fees; they can also let you know what kind of contractor is required for each phase of construction, but the general contractor orders most of the building materials based on your approval and hires subcontractors and tradesmen such as carpenters, plumbers, electricians, and roofers. A general contractor who owns a large company may have his or her own crew consisting of employees who have passed qualifying examinations for the fields in which they specialize.

- **Subcontractors** specialize in a particular field and work on their own. They are generally hired by the general contractor to perform a specific job like plumbing, masonry, and wiring. The general contractor signs an agreement with them, and he or she pays them for their services according to the initial estimate the subcontractors provided. Your local Building and Safety Department might require a subcontractor licensure, depending on state laws.

The Contract

The contract should protect the rights of both parties and specify the scope and limitations of the work to be performed, payment, method of payment, and payment schedules. For major construction projects, such as building a house, payment should be "cost-plus" or "time and materials." The contractor is paid for the cost of labor and materials plus a percent of that cost, which ranges between 10 percent and 25 percent.

A general contractor's agreement[12] normally includes the central agreements, plans, material specifications, permits, code requirements, notice of rescission, and much more. Generally, a contractor will provide his or her own contract, but you would want an experienced construction lawyer to review it before you sign it. If you haven't already, hire a lawyer who specializes in tort law to review all contracts and agreements, even if you've written them yourself. The local bar association will provide a list of lawyers who specialize in construction matters, and in some states a referral from the bar association will lower the cost for initial consultations.

What to Include in a Construction Contract

Some states have model contracts, but not all of them cover important topics. Generally, the following items should be included in a contract:

- Contractor's name, address, and license or registration (if required by law). Be careful if the address is a P.O. Box.

- The date when the job will start and the completion dates for different phases. This is very important if your lender makes disbursements based on stage completions.

[12]See sample of General Contractor's Agreement on Appendix C

- Detailed description of products and materials that will be used.

- Payment schedule.

- Final payment and conditions.

- Warranties.

- Contractor guarantee.

- Permits and fees. This clause has to mention all applicable permits the contractor has to pull and, in the case of subcontractors, the ones pertaining to them.

- What kind of subcontractors the contractor intends to hire.

- Insurance coverage for the contractor's crew. If the contractor hires subcontractors, they must have their own workmen's compensation liability.

- Contractor's injury or damage liability.

- Provision for future changes to the contract.

- Contractor's responsibility to perform the cleanup after the construction is completed.

- Use or return to supplier of unused products and materials.

- Notice of recission. Under federal law you have three days to give written notice to the contractor of your decision to cancel the contract.

- Arbitration clause. This clause should state that the American Arbitration Association (AAA) (**www.adr.org**) is the settlement intermediary if there is a dispute. The AAA is a not-for-profit organization that is committed to help resolve disputes by arbitration in different consumer areas, including construction. Specifying this organization would be less expensive than retaining the services of a private attorney. Some local offices of the Better Business Bureau also settle disputes by arbitration.

- A clause protecting against property liens. If the general contractor fails to pay one of the hired subcontractors, then that subcontractor can legally file a lien on your property. A recommended practice is to include lien waivers signed by each one of the parties that is scheduled to perform work or supply materials. It is the general contractor's responsibility to obtain the waivers, completed and signed for inclusion in the contract.

Payment

You will need to establish a payment schedule in order to maintain control over the completion of each phase of construction as well as over the remaining balance of the project total. The contract should specify dates of completion on significant stages in the construction process. The general recommendation is to associate payments with the satisfactory completion of each phase of construction. See the next section for a better understanding of each phase of construction and the scope of work in each that will determine payment and a payment schedule.

It is normal for the contractor to ask for a deposit before construction begins. The deposit usually covers the cost of materials required to begin the job but may cover other startup costs. Contractors commonly request from 10 percent to 20 percent of the total to be paid up front; however, some states have put a limit on the percentage that the contractor can request as a deposit.

Scope of Work

In building construction, everything depends on something else, and you will have to be dedicated to each phase of the project if it is to progress smoothly. Mistakes are costly, but delays are even more so. Understanding each phase of the project is essential in planning and during construction.

1. **Support:** Nonconstruction costs related to a project, such as insurance, permits, portable toilets, dumpsters, administrative expenses, and other miscellaneous expenses are part of the total cost of building the home. Be sure you know what the general contractor includes in this category of expenditures.

2. **Site Work:** This phase pertains to the preliminary excavation, filling, and leveling that must be done before the actual construction begins. Ensure that the contractor has contacted local authorities and utility companies to determine if any municipal or company utility lines run under or near the house.

3. **Concrete:** Foundations, footings, and floor slabs are the common uses of concrete, but you might also need it for pools, walks, or curbs. Inclement weather, always a factor in construction, can delay this important phase because

concrete requires specific temperatures and dry weather to cure.

4. **Masonry:** Often required to install brick or block foundations, fireplaces, or other structural or veneer surfaces.

5. **Metalwork:** Steel or aluminum framing or decorative metal elements may be required to meet codes or design specifications.

6. **Wood and Plastics:** Wood framing, sub-flooring, roof decking, and patio decks are usually required, but also shelving and finished carpentry such as kitchen cabinetry.

7. **Water Systems:** Plumbing and septic systems are installed early in the construction process.

8. **Electrical Systems:** This is the central nervous system of your house and includes electrical service, controls, lighting, outlets, thermostats, and fire prevention systems. Building codes tightly restrict how electrical service is installed, but you should discuss with your contractor where certain connections and electrical functions should be placed.

9. **Heating and Cooling:** Furnaces, air ducts (if forced-air heating), vents, and central air conditioning should be installed before drywall or plaster cover the wall frames.

10. **Thermal and Moisture Protection:** Any new house will need to have insulation, waterproofing, sealing, siding, and other materials that protect the interior

from the elements. Insulation should be installed in the walls, ceilings beneath the attic or crawl space, and in the basement ceiling. Exterior wall covering, or siding, is a major decision, whether you choose stucco, brick, clapboard, aluminum, vinyl, or any other material because it greatly affects initial costs and long-term maintenance costs.

11. **Interior and Exterior Finishing:** This involves finishing materials for walls, floors, ceilings, countertops, woodwork, and nearly every other surface in and on the home.

12. **Mechanical Systems:** Garage door openers, ceiling fans, fixtures, and other amenities.

13. **Furnishings:** Generally, only built-in furnishings are included in the construction process; interior design is usually left for later unless the contractor offers a more inclusive service.

14. **Landscaping and Access:** The contractor may oversee the construction of exterior retaining walls, landscaping, installation of asphalt driveways, and other exterior finishing work.

How to Make Sure the Job is Done Right

Staying involved and dedicated to the project is the best way to get the job done right. When you build your own home, you are the boss, but rely on the contractor for suggestions regarding choice of materials, methods of construction and planning for unexpected events. Always ask about alternative materials or products, but respect the contractor's experience using those products and dealing with their suppliers.

If the home is a custom design, your architect may have recommended certain products when designing the home so don't hesitate to ask why those materials were suggested. Acceptable alternatives may be more cost-effective for you.

Buy the International Building Code (also available at most libraries) which includes detailed guides for every step involved in a construction project and discusses materials and specifications that comply with building codes.

THE COST OF BUILDING YOUR OWN HOME

In this section you will learn how to buy land, develop your house plans, estimate building costs, identify ways to save on various costs, select subcontractors for specific jobs, negotiate contracts, buy materials, and establish schedules for your workers and yourself.

Acquiring Land

As Will Rogers said, "Buy land; they don't make it anymore." But finding a suitable property is sometimes difficult. In urban areas, vacant lots are rare or are very expensive, so choice based on location is limited. Suburban properties or rural land offers greater choices but may dictate the necessity to commute to services or place of employment and may distance you from family and friends. The help of a real estate professional may be invaluable when searching for available land.

Land purchases present some unique problems. Zoning regulations may have categorized seemingly desirable properties as flood plains or some other prohibiting classification. Some municipalities require that a minimum number of acres must be included in the sale. Soil tests to determine its suitability for both supporting a structure and providing drainage are often required, particularly in rural areas where there are no municipal sewage systems or water supplies, so that homeowners must install septic tanks and drill wells. A refund provision contingent upon suitability for a septic tank and drainage and upon availability of deep-well water may be required in the purchase contract. Your local health department may conduct this test, saving you a lot of money.

The price of land varies greatly from area to area and depends on many factors, most of which relate to the three rules of choosing a home: location, location, location. How much you can afford within your overall budget, however, depends on your projected construction cost, usually measured in dollars per square foot, your budget, and the size of the home you wish to build. If you've decided on a total budget of $200,000, for example, and construction costs in your area average $100 per foot for a home of 1,320 square feet, you can afford to pay as much as $68,000 for the land.

A landowner may take a note in lieu of payment of all or part of the purchase price of his land, legally subordinating his interest in that land in a Land Contract to your lender. Essentially, you would possess the land but would not be the only owner. Though a legal alternative to an outright purchase, a land contract can create problems. Land contracts will be discussed further in Chapter 7, and a sample of a Land Contract is included in Appendix C.

How to Develop Your House Plans

When considering a construction loan to build your home, lenders will look for assurances that the project can be completed and that the terms of all laws and regulations will be met. You will have to present yourself as someone well-organized and knowledgeable about the construction process. In Chapter 7 more will be said about how to secure a construction loan, but for now it's important to know what choices the lenders may offer or require for managing the project funds:

- A contract bid, already discussed in a previous section.

- The "cost-plus" contract or a fixed-price contract. A general contractor may estimate the cost of building your home by averaging subcontractor bids, totaling the averages, and adding 20 percent of the total to cover overhead and profit. You should add to this, if the contractor has not, the cost of architectural services for designing the home, which may range between $2,000 and $4,000.

- A manager's contract is useful when you are taking over most of the responsibilities of a general contractor and is an arrangement that you make with a general contractor who is given sole responsibility to act as your manager with subcontractors. The general contractor will limit his charges to 20 percent to 30 percent of the usual charges for general contracting services. The general contractor will help with locating subcontractors, setting up schedules, checking for quality of work and materials used, and he will order materials on your behalf, if necessary. You have the responsibility to secure suppliers and permits, pay suppliers and subcontractors, order inspections, and declare job acceptance. It is prudent to retain legal services to review a manager's contract; an example of a manager's contract in included in Appendix C.

Estimating Building Costs

Before breaking down the detailed costs of building your home, you will need to know the general costs of building a home in your area.

- Real Estate agents have access to information about comparable homes built in any area and can provide you with information about homes that have been built in the previous four-month period.

- The local tax office (assessor) may have additional information and many public records listing the details of home sales in the area. Information regarding the square feet of the house, the lot size, and the last recorded value — in most cases, the last sales price — are usually part of the record.

- Talk with a local contractor who will know costs per square foot in your area.

To have a more defined cost estimate, use the following worksheet by filling out each item based on subcontractor's bids under the "Budget" column. Later you can use the same form to track expenditures during the course of construction and to compare actual expenditures to your budget details.

BREAKDOWN ITEMS	NOTES	Material	Labor	Budget	Difference
1. Plans and permits					
2. Site preparation					
3. Meter/Service moves					
4. Concrete foundations					
5. Concrete flat work					
6. Masonry					
7. Plumbing					
8. Electrical					
9. Phone/TV/computer					
10. AC and heating					
11. Carpentry					
12. Framing lumber					
13. Roofing					
14. Fireplace					
15. Sheet metal					
16. Gutters					
17. Ornamental iron					
18. Deck coating					
19. Exterior siding					
20. Insulation					
21. Drywall					
22. Overhead garage door					
23. Cabinets (kitchen, bathrooms, garage)					
24. Laminated plastic					
25. Ceramic tile					
26. Marble					
27. Glazing for windows					
28. Windows and doors					
29. Carpentry (finish)					
30. Finish material (trims, crowns)					
31. Painting					

32. Floor coverings				
33. Appliances				
34. Fencing				
35. Landscaping/sprinklers				
36. Scaffolding				
37. Exterior stucco				
38. Equipment rental				
39. Clean-up and dump				
40.				
41.				
42.				
43.				
44.				
45. Subtotal *Add items 1 thru 44*				
46. Contingency *Multiply item 45x %*				
47. Supervision *Add items 46 & 46, x %*				
48. Net Cost *Add Items 45 thru 47*				

To calculate the total estimate, you will have to add the cost of the land to the total cost. The result will be your total project cost (land and construction).

WHERE TO GET INFORMATION

- **Plans and Permits.** If you decide to retain services from an architect, he or she will have to give you an estimated cost before beginning work. The fee schedules for permits are available at your local Safety and Building Department. Some municipalities provide prepared booklets explaining necessary requirements for plans, required permits, and inspection procedures for owners.

- **Site Preparation.** This is the preliminary excavation, filling, and leveling of the site that has to be done before the construction work begins. Excavation companies are listed in the yellow pages, or, if you have a manager, he or she can give you referrals.

- **Utility and Service Connections.** This pertains to connection of the power, sewer, and water services. If your lot is in an undeveloped area, this can involve considerable expense because you may have to pay for extending water or electrical lines, including the poles. Contact local utility providers for power and municipal agencies for both water and sewer connections. Your plumber will install the connection, but you have to pay the fee to the county. If you need a septic system, contact a subcontractor specializing in the installation of septic tanks and drainage fields.

- **Concrete Foundation and Masonry.** This is the masonry base on which the construction will rest. A mason or concrete subcontractor handles this job.

- **Concrete Flat Work.** This includes finished slabs in

garage and basement floors, as well as patios, driveways, and walks left with a rough surface. Your concrete subcontractor will quote the job per square foot.

- **Plumbing.** The plumber should install all pipes and necessary fixtures like sinks, toilets, and water heater. Appliances are not included.

- **Electrical.** This includes interior and exterior wiring throughout the house according to local building codes. The bid should include all switches, receptacles, wires, panels, and breakers as well as special wiring and set-up for appliances.

- **Carpentry and Framing.** A "rough-in" carpenter builds framing, joist, sub-flooring, roof trusses, decks, and other unfinished wooden structures. The bid must be based on square footage. A lumber company will provide quotes on lumber and will usually offer contractor discounts on larger purchases.

- **Roofing.** A roofing subcontractor can familiarize you with the choices of roofing materials and their lifespans, all of which affect the price. Materials are usually quoted per square yard and labor per square foot.

- **Fireplace.** Fireplaces have changed a geat deal over the years. Most have been built out of brick or stone by masons, but in recent years prefabricated fireplaces and manufactured inserts are used in combination with wood construction housing a stovepipe. These may be installed by carpenters.

- **Deck Coating.** If you choose to have a deck, it will need a special coating to protect it from the elements. A house painter normally performs this job.

- **Exterior Siding.** Siding may be clapboard, vinyl or metal siding, stucco, or other material. The subcontractor installing siding depends on the material used.

- **Insulation.** Insulation is installed within the walls to create a thermal barrier that helps maintain a constant temperature inside the house. Companies specializing in insulating homes normally perform this job.

- **Drywall.** Drywall is the modern version of a plaster wall. It is available in four by eight sheets and is cut to size to cover frames, smoothed with tape and spread compound, and sanded for a finished wall surface that can then be painted or covered with wallpaper. Drywall specialists perform this job.

- **Cabinets.** Cabinets may be custom-built or prefabricated. Finishing carpenters will provide you with a bid on materials and labor if custom-built. Prefabricated cabinets can be installed by subcontractors of the store from which they're purchased or by your own subcontractors.

- **Windows and Doors**. A finish carpenter is the subcontractor that will do this job, but if the supplier has installation specialists, ask them to give you a quote for labor and windows, doors, door casings, trim moldings, and upper wall moldings.

- **Driveway.** Concrete, asphalt, pavestone, brick, and other materials are used. Specialists who work with each of these materials will perform this job.

- **Painting.** A professional painter will provide suggestions for materials and a bid for both labor and materials, including primers, paints, textured materials, and other products. This is one area where do-it-yourselfers can save money, and much of the work can be done after occupancy.

- **Floor Coverings.** Floor coverings might include wood, carpet, vinyl, tile, or others. Prices vary considerably, as do levels of quality. Installation is often done by the suppliers and is included in an inclusive bid.

- **Appliances.** Appliances are among the last items installed and depend greatly on both your budget and lifestyle. Energy Star units, rated for greater efficiency and thus lower operating costs, may be more expensive initially but will save you money in the long run.

WORK SCHEDULES

Work schedules must be associated with each phase of construction, not only to map progress of the construction but because your lender will likely peg construction loan disbursements to the completion of each phase. You will have to lay out a schedule for the completion of each task and phase of construction taking into account the unexpected, like inclement weather.

Following is the sequence of steps usually followed in constructing a house:

1. **Laying out preliminary lines for the lot and house.** A land survey is required, either commissioned by you or from an existing survey on file with the assessor's office. If you have financed the purchase of your land, the escrow company will have to give the lender a preliminary title report for the land that includes the survey. (This step will be explained in more detail in the following chapter.) The dimensions of the house should be laid out on a copy of the survey map for use by the excavation and footing contractors. Local regulations will dictate clearance distances from streets, adjoining properties, and overhanging objects. The house should face in the same direction as other houses on your side of the street.

2. **Clearing and excavation of the lot.** It may be necessary to clear rocks or trees before excavating the lot, but remember that trees provide beauty and shade, mitigate erosion, and increase the real estate value of the property. Tree removal companies specialize in removing trees without damaging surrounding trees, and heavy equipment contractors that specialize in homesite preparation are the proper choices for excavation.

3. **Connection of utilities.** It's your job to handle the administrative procedures for intiating service. Contact your local utilities and schedule your services once installations of the electrical wiring, plumbing, sewage, and gas lines are complete. You will need to schedule a disruption of electrical service to install the proper connections, and your electrical subcontractor will have to install a temporary electrical panel that must be inspected to ensure it meets local codes. Both well

and septic systems, if required, must be inspected after installation and before use.

4. **Pouring the footing.** A footing is the support upon which the foundation rests. It is the first step in a two-stage process when building a foundation, and it is critical to the structural integrity of the entire house. Concrete masons install the footing after laying out the dimensions of the house on the lot. Once the concrete in the footing is cured and inspected, the foundation is built on it out of concrete or block.

5. **Building the foundation.** Code requirements for foundations vary a lot within the country, but generally the foundation wall has to rise to at least six inches above grade (surface of the adjoining soil), high enough to divert water away from the house so that the wood siding and framing is protected from moisture in the soil. The type of foundation — full cellar or crawl space-- will be determined in your plans, but the walls for a full cellar must be a minimum of seven feet between floor and ceiling in the basement. Your finished foundation will also have to be waterproofed on the exterior by professional companies that specialize in working with waterproofing materials. Finally, most lenders and code requirements require soil tests to prove there are no pest infections. The seller of the lot should have given you the soil test report; if you don't have one, you must hire a professional to perform this test.

6. **Installing initial plumbing.** Once the foundation is constructed, but before the basement floor is poured in, the plumbing subcontractor must install the sewer line

and the water pipes that will run beneath the concrete.

7. **Pouring the slab on grade.** This is the concrete that will surround the perimeter of the house; you will have to call for an inspection before pouring the concrete.

8. **Framing walls, joists, and trusses.** Framing carpenters will give shape to the house in this phase as they build its skeleton, so to speak. Orders for lumber in various dimensions, nails, and other hardware will have to be made as needed so no time is lost.

9. **Exterior siding**. Underlayments, roof decking, siding, and brick or stone veneers are all constructed during this phase, while interior work proceeds on other phases of the project.

10. **Chimneys and roofing**. The chimney and cricket or saddle must be constructed before the roofing materials are installed.

11. **Installing electrical wiring and inner-wall plumbing.** All the electrical installation, plumbing pipes, and heating and AC ducts must be installed before the walls are covered with drywall. All installations will have to be inspected.

12. **Installing insulation.** Insulation also has to be put in place before the walls, floors, and ceilings are covered.

13. **Installing drywall.** Usually, residential house walls are made with drywall or sheetrock (gypsum). Drywall subcontractors perform this job. After drywall is attached to the frames, spaces between panels will have to be

filled with compound and tape and sanded smooth. In bathrooms and other areas where moisture might collect, a special drywall that is resistant to moisture is used.

14. **Installing interior trim.** This step refers to the installation of doors, moldings, cabinets, and shelves in pantry or closet spaces.

15. **Installing floor coverings.** The covering on floors in the kitchen and bathrooms can be done at this stage, as well as the vinyl underlayment. Carpeting and other fine coverings should only be installed following painting and the installation of doors and trim. Be sure to allow clearance over carpeting for doors that open over it.

16. **Painting interior walls and trim.** Unless you have decided to do this step yourself, the painting subcontractor will paint the interior.

17. **Installing fixtures.** Fixtures include bathtubs, showers, sinks, faucets, and other connections to the plumbing; receptacles, outlets, switches, lighting, and other connections to the electrical wiring; as well as controls for heating, air conditioning, and appliances.

18. **Cleaning up.** All contractors should include cleaning up after their own work as part of their bids, but there is always more to do, and you may wish to do this work yourself at this point.

19. **Finishing and covering floors.** Hardwood flooring, if installed, should be finished while no other workers are present for both aesthetic and safety reasons. Dust raised by other workers can easily become embedded in

the finish, and the finishes themselves emit dangerous vapors and can be volatile until dry. Carpet installers are usually contracted by the supplier.

20. **Installing a driveway.** All heavy work should be completed before the installation of the driveway. Because base layers of stone or gravel will not be completely settled and packed, and some materials like concrete and asphalt that have to cure over time will not yet be capable of withstanding heavy traffic, no work requiring heavy trucks or other vehicles should be left undone before installation of the driveway.

21. **Landscaping the property.** Minimally, the surrounding land should be graded and seeded to prevent runoff and erosion, but landscaping features can be done incrementally after occupancy to spread out the cost. If you choose to complete landscaping during construction, licensed landscapers will provide complete services including the purchase of plants, trees, stone for walls and walks, and more.

22. **Final inspections**. Upon completion of the structure, both the local authorities and your lender will make inspections of the main systems to ensure they meet codes and other building regulations.

Each of the preceding stages of construction is important, not only to map out the progress and work schedules of the project, but also to satisfy your lender's requirements for disbursement of funds when a project is self-managed.

PERMITS AND INSPECTIONS

Permits

Specific building regulations vary from state to state and may be complicated by local codes and regulations. Normally, you will receive a package of pertinent information[13] which may include detailed instructions on how to apply for a building permit; guidelines and regulations regarding plans and clearances; and materials lists for certain components of the house, especially for footings, foundations, basements, and framing.

Inspections

The local building and safety departments should also include in their informational packets the types of inspections that have to be made and a schedule of when they must be made. Most contractors have this information and will know from experience that work cannot be continued until completed work passes building inspections. As manager, however, you must ensure inspections are made and corrections made if needed. Inspections may be required for:

- Temporary electrical or saw service, to ensure proper grounding.

- Footings, to ensure they are strong enough to support the foundation and house structure.

- Slab, before concrete is poured, and any plumbing installation within the slab.

- Electrical, plumbing, heating and air conditioning wiring before the drywall is installed.

- Structural framing, to ensure its integrity after wiring for electrical, plumbing, and HVAC is completed.

- Insulation.

- Final electrical, plumbing, HVAC, and general building to make sure they work properly, comply with codes, and are safe.

CONTINGENCY FUND

Earlier, the Cost Breakdown Worksheet listed detailed items that should be included in your budget calculations. As with all things, not every expense can be predicted and it is only prudent to include in your calculations some provision for expenses that normally reveal themselves later in the construction process or cannot be foreseen, like changes in the weather.

The worksheet does include budget item 46, contingency, which is a percent of the budget total. Commonly, that figure is in the range of 5 percent to 10 percent of the total cost estimate, including contractor's profit and overhead. If you estimated that the construction on your house would cost you $75,000, for example, your contingency fund might be $7,000, or 9 percent of the total.

[13]See Appendix C for a sample municipal package.

At this point, it is instructive to look at expenses that might only appear as construction progresses or which force modifications to original estimates due to unforeseen circumstances:

- Attorney fees.

- Builder's risk or fire insurance.

- Contractor's profit and overhead (if you decided to hire a contractor).

- Additional architectural and design fees for changes in plans ordered by county.

- Power and water consumption.

- Equipment rental (if subcontractors don't provide certain equipment needed).

- Delays due to weather, damages, failure to meet terms of regulatory compliance, or contractor error.

Home buying is a process with many steps.

5

UNDERSTANDING THE HOME BUYING PROCESS

ESCROW

What is Escrow?

Escrow acts to protect all parties during the period of preparation and processing of all necessary documentation needed to close the deal on the purchase. Funds are held in escrow by agreement and are disbursed by the escrow company as terms of agreement are met or at closing.

You role as the borrower/buyer: get loan approval, examine seller's disclosures, sign escrow instructions, get home inspections and appraisal, acquire hazard insurance, and review and sign the identification sheet.

Role of the title company: acquire the preliminary report for the property, which includes the name of the current owner, the legal description of the property, and the survey (indicating the lines of the lot and its location). The title company also reports a 24-month title history for the property, usually known as "Chain of Title."

Role of the escrow company: acquire signatures to the escrow instructions, which is basically a document instructing the escrow holder (escrow company or attorney) to compile all pertinent documents with signatures of both seller and buyer, if required, and to disburse funds at the close of escrow (COE) to all parties involved in the process, including the seller, real estate agents for both the seller and buyer, and the mortgage broker. Your real estate agent will have to open escrow with the company or attorney designated in the purchase contract. In western states, the escrow and title companies are the same and fulfill both roles.

During the period of escrow, typically stated in the purchase contract as from 30-45 days, you must find a lender to fund your purchase. Escrow is initiated after the purchase contract is fully executed (signed by all parties).

Whether you work with a mortgage broker who will search the market for the most suitable lender or directly with the loan processor at the lending company itself, the intended purchase must be funded at close of escrow dated on your purchase contract. Only under special circumstances should the period of escrow be extended.

TITLE COMPANY

Title companies are incorporated businesses that provide services to real estate agents, lenders, and individuals (in this case, a buyer). They perform the title search and submit a report that might include any irregularities that might affect transfer of ownership. Title companies may also be escrow holders in some cases. Fees must be disclosed to you prior to the lender's Good Faith Estimate and may include:

- Title insurance, which protects you and the lender against errors or omissions made by the person who performed the title search. This fee is normally calculated based on the sales price and is paid only once.

- Escrow fees, which are charges for being the escrow holder.

- Document preparation fees.

- Courier fees.

- Recording fees charged by the local county clerk or recorder for recording your title and loan.

- Tax stamps.

- School taxes.

Title Search

Every lender will ask for the title search to ensure that you are buying the property from the person who actually owns the house. A title search consists of an examination of the property's chain of ownership for the last 24 months. The title search varies from state to state depending on the records kept, but the public records that may affect the title of a property include records of death, divorces, court judgments, liens, property taxes, and wills.

Title Report

The Title Report is the summary of the title search; it must include the chain of title and the following topics:

- Vesting of title.

- Legal description.

- Current assessment records.

- Property tax information.

- Mechanics liens.

- Current deed status of all mortgages.

- Judgments.

- Federal tax liens.

- Any customized information that the lender may require.

Required Documentation

Provided by the escrow company:

- **Escrow instructions.** This document shows how the escrow will be handled and the time of its closing. It becomes an addendum to the purchase agreement, stating that the signatories (seller and buyer) are employing the escrow company or attorney to act as escrow agent and title agent (if applicable) in connection with the transaction. It also authorizes the agent to close escrow based upon the terms of said agreement and any subsequent modifications. It normally includes explanations and managing details for the following:

- Instructions and details on the title report and title insurance.

- How the Title will be transferred and which legal documents will be needed for you to have the property deed in your name.

- Payment of encumbrances, liens, or charges in case the title search reveals that any are recorded (generally, it is the responsibility of the seller to make payment to clean the title).

- Transfer of personal property.

- Commission disbursement.

- How the funds must be deposited (certified funds or cashier's check).

- Date for close of escrow.

- Cancellation.

- Resignation of escrow agent.

- Copies to third parties.

- Corrections.

- Notices.

- Supplemental taxes.

- Post closing adjustments.

- Corroboration of expenses assigned to both the seller and the buyer as stated in the purchase agreement (seller to pay owner's policy of title insurance, half of the escrow fee, recording and reconveyances fees related to any existing lien, the real property transfer tax, the home protection plan, and any other loan charges specified by FHA or VA as mandatory seller costs, when applicable, and buyer to pay American Land Title Association (ALTA) policy of title insurance, loan fees as required by the lender, half of the escrow fee, and recording fees for the deed and mortgage).

- **Compliance agreement.** This document is signed by both the seller and the buyer who agree to cooperate fully in the execution of any documents deemed necessary to address an adjustment, error or omission in documentation related to this transaction or is deemed necessary or desirable by the escrow company. All parties must also agree to pay any amounts necessary to fulfill the company's obligations which are payable to any of the parties named in the purchase contract, lending instructions, escrow instructions, or any other instruction considered part of the transaction, including unpaid or delinquent taxes and any shortages of funds that would prohibit the proper disbursement of funds and closing escrow.

- **Escrow Disclaimer.** Explains that the escrow agent's role is to act as a neutral third party, to provide respective instructions for each party to a transaction, and to prepare relevant documentation necessary to complete the purchase contract. Since its role is one of impartiality, the escrow agent cannot act as an attorney and cannot advise the parties to any legal remedy in response to the consequences of any instrument prepared in connection with the transaction.

- **Statement of Identity.**[14] This statement is signed by each party involved in the transaction (seller and buyer), and by both husband and wife (if applicable) before a policy of title insurance can be issued and the title can be recorded. Information you must provide includes legal names including your spouse's maiden name, date of marriage, residences and employment history during the preceding 10 years, any former marriages and reasons for their termination, as well as the address of the subject property, required to record the title.

The statement is provided by the mortgage broker, lender, bank, or credit union.[15]

- **Uniform Loan Application.** Form 1003, a standard form issued by Freddie Mac, lists all information on the property you want to buy, the type of mortgage, and buyer's information, including but not limited to:

  - Legal name.

  - Social security number.

---

[14]See sample in Appendix C

[15]Samples of all the forms described here are provided in Appendix C

- Date of birth.

- Marital status.

- Dependents.

- Present address and previous addresses if you've lived at your current address for less than two years .

- Your employment information.

- Monthly income and your housing expenses (rent).

- Assets and liabilities.

- Declarations regarding judgments, foreclosure, lawsuits, or delinquency on any federal debts or any other loan or financial obligation including alimony and/or child support.

- Information for government monitoring purposes regarding ethnicity, race, and gender.

Form 1003 also lists transaction details such as the purchase price, estimated closing costs, down payment, loan amount, and total estimated funds needed for closing.

- **Borrower Signature Authorization.** A document authorizing the lender or broker to verify your past and present employment earnings records, bank accounts, and any other asset balances that are needed to process your loan application. It also allows them to order a credit report and verify credit information including landlord references.

- **Borrower's Certification and Authorization.** This

document certifies that you have applied for a mortgage loan and that you have completed a loan application containing various information regarding the purpose of the loan, the amount and source of the down-payment, as well as information about employment, income, assets, and liabilities. It also certifies that the information you provided is true and complete and that you understand the consequences of providing false information. In addition, it authorizes the lender or broker to verify the information you provide.

- **Disclosure Notices.** A release of buyer information, referred to as the "affidavit of occupancy anti-coercion statement" for insurance purposes, to meet the terms of the Fair Credit Reporting Act, and to satisfy disclosure provisions required of FHA loans if applicable.

- **Equal Credit Opportunity Act.** This document explains to you that the Federal Equal Credit Opportunity Act prohibits creditors from discriminating against credit applicants on the basis of race, color, religion, national origin, sex, marital status, or age. It may be given to you because all or part of your income derives from any public assistance program or because you have in good faith exercised any right under the Consumer Credit Protection Act.

- **The Housing Financial Discrimination Act of 1977 Fair Lending Notice.** Similar to the ECOA, described above.

- **Mortgage Loan Origination Agreement.** The content of this form varies from state to state. It is used in the event you have employed the services of a mortgage broker. By signing, you are agreeing to pay the broker compensation for his or her services.

- **Privacy Policy Disclosure**. This form explains how the confidentiality of your personal information is protected, what kind of information the lender or broker will share, the reason for sharing that information, and with whom it will be shared. You may choose to prohibit the lender or broker from sharing information with non-affiliated third parties, affiliates, and others. You may also elect not to have them contact you offering products or services by mail or telephone.

- **Notice to Applicant of Right to Receive Copy of Appraisal Report.** This document states that you have the right to receive a copy of the appraisal for the house. You have 90 days after the lender or broker notifies you of the action taken on your loan application to make a written request for the report.

- **Servicing Disclosure Statement.** Subsequent to approval of your mortgage loan, the mortgage loan may be sold or transferred to a different lender. This is a very common practice in the mortgage industry, but you have rights that protect you in the event the original or new lender does not give you 15 days written notice before the effective date of the transfer.

- **Tax Information Authorization and Request for Copy or Transcript of Tax form.** You will be required to sign both forms allowing the lender or broker to report specified information to the IRS in case you have tax liens or federal debts.

- **Variable Rate Mortgage Program Disclosure.** If your loan is an Adjustable Rate Mortgage, this form explains in detail how it works and when the initial rate will change. Adjustable Rate Mortgages will be discussed further in Chapter 7.

- **USA Patriot Act Disclosure.** This is a form that certifies the authenticity of your personal information. This is a recent requirement in keeping with the terms of the Patriot Act of 2005.

- **Appraisal Order Form.** By signing this form, you give the lender or broker authorization to order an appraisal on your behalf for the purpose of establishing a fair market value for the home you are buying, and it also states that the appraisal report will be forwarded to the lender to support the value of the property in question. You must prepay the appraisal fee unless the purchase contract establishes that the seller is responsible for this expense.

- **FACT Act Credit Score and Risk Based Pricing Disclosure.** This form will be provided to you after the lender or broker has pulled your credit report. Lenders, brokers, banks, and credit unions commonly use specialized credit-report agencies that provide, in a single summarized report, credit information on file at the three main credit-reporting agencies (Experian, Equifax, and TransUnion). This disclosure is the instrument used by the lender or broker to report the credit score issued by each of the credit reporting agencies as well as that issued by the credit reporting agency providing the summarized report. Risk-based pricing disclosures are issued by the same credit agency that reports your credit scores. They indicate the lender's risk in awarding you a loan. You are entitled to an explanation from the loan officer handling your loan application on how the credit scores may affect the interest rate for your loan.

All the above-mentioned paperwork may vary from state to state and be different for FHA and VA guaranteed loans.

It is important to mention that you must read and fully understand all documents given to you for signature. Never sign a document or form that is not filled in completely, especially if it involves paying fees or expenses up front. Schedule appointments for signing documents very carefully and allow sufficient time so that you can review all documents and ask any questions that will help you understand the scope and meaning of any parts of the documents presented. If you feel incapable of comprehending financial and legal documents, consider retaining the services of a lawyer who can explain the implications of the documents and what they mean to you. The cost of retaining a lawyer is easily offset by the avoidance of legal problems later.

PROCEDURES	COMMENTS
Loan prequalification	The lender/broker will issue a pre-qualification document.
Loan application (Form 1003)	Your lender will provide this form and assist you in filling it out.
Credit report	You are entitled to a copy.
Pre-approval from lender representative (If working with a mortgage broker, the processor will have to submit the loan application and credit report to two or three lenders.)	The response time is usually 24-48 hrs; the loan officer must notify you.
Sign the Good Faith Estimate, Truth in Lending, and disclosures (GFE and TIL will be explained in Chapter 7).	The lender/broker has to issue the GFE and TIL within three days of your signing the loan application.
Supporting documentation	Depending on the loan program for which you qualify, the loan officer will ask for supporting documentation that may include pay-stubs, bank statements, identification, and more.
Verification	The loan processor will verify supporting information regarding employment, residence, and finances.
Review of purchase contract and supporting actions	The loan processor will review the purchase contract and will order an appraisal, preliminary title search, and quotes for hazard insurance. If the purchase contract stipulates that you will pay the appraisal, payment must made up-front.
Submission of application for approval	Once all criteria for the loan are met, the full loan application will be submitted to underwriting for approval. Depending on the lender, this may take two to five days, but the underwriter may need additional or revised information prior to submission to the title company.

Locking interest rates	During all the previous stages, your rate will be floating, which means the rate given in the GFE and TIL is an estimate that may change daily. The locked rate may be higher or lower but is guaranteed for a declared period of time.
Submission to title company	The title company begins documentation preparation.
Revisions	Processor will fulfill any additional conditions requested by underwriting prior to funding. Your loan officer may ask you for additional information needed to satisfy other lenders' conditions.
Submission to escrow company	The lender must submit documents to the escrow company, and the estimated HUD is provided by escrow.
Funding Approval	The loan officer will notify you when your loan is funded and will indicate available dates for the closing, as well as funds necessary at time of closing.
Closing	The loan officer or realtor must be present at the signing of documents.
Funding	The signed documents are resubmitted to the lender, who arranges funding within 24-48 hrs.
Notification to record transactions	The escrow company receives word from the lender to prepare deed and mortgage loan documents for the public record.
The property is yours!	The escrow company will have ready a closing package that must include your recorded deed, note, HUD I, and reimbursement of any funds. Once the files are recorded, you own the property.

HOMEOWNER'S INSURANCE

Why You Must Get Hazard Insurance

The main reason for getting hazard insurance is that lenders want to be sure their investment is protected. Your property will become the collateral on the mortgage. If something happens to the house, the lender may not be able to recover the loan if the property is not covered by an insurance policy.

Depending on the lender's requirements, hazard insurance must cover either the cost of replacement or the amount of the loan amount (not the down payment). Coverage must be for damages or loss due to:

- Fire or lightning.

- Windstorm or hail.

- Explosion.

- Riot or civil commotion.

- Aircraft and vehicles.

- Smoke, if loss is sudden and accidental.

- Vandalism.

- Theft.

- Falling objects.

- Weight of ice, snow, or sleet which causes damage to property contained in a building.

- Collapse of a dwelling or any part of a dwelling.

- Sudden and accidental discharge or overflow of water or steam from within a plumbing, heating, or air conditioning system, or from within a household appliance, but not for deterioration, rust, mold, or wet or dry rot due to the presence of water over a period of time.

- Sudden and accidental tearing apart, cracking, burning or bulging of a steam, hot water, or air conditioning system, or appliance for heating water.

- Freezing of a plumbing, heating, or air conditioning system, or household appliance.

- Sudden and accidental damage from artificially generated electrical current.

The coverage excludes floods, earthquakes, and mudslides.

Shopping Around for Hazard Insurance

Hazard insurance is classified according to the type of property being insured, and you should familiarize yourself with the types of coverage that apply to your intended home. The complexities of home insurance coverage are beyond the scope of this book, but there are some basic concepts everyone should know when shopping for home insurance, particularly how claims are paid. Your lender may require certain types of coverage.

Insurance companies reimburse for losses in three principal ways: full replacement, guaranteed replacement, or cash value.

- Full Replacement guarantees that the insurance company will pay for replacement to the limit of coverage.

- Guaranteed Cost guarantees that the insurer will rebuild your house no matter the cost.

- Cash Value Insurance guarantees that the insurance company will pay an amount equal to the current market value of the house.

The scope of your coverage, keeping in mind the lender's requirements, should be discussed with your insurance agent after you have decided on the best quote from several companies. There can be considerable differences in the quotes received, depending on the number of claims recently made against each company and the structure of their products. Contact your state insurance regulatory agency to research licensed insurers and the number of complaints filed against each.

It is your decision, also, regarding deductibles (out-of-pocket expenses for any damages) which might keep your premiums a bit lower.

If you are working with a mortgage broker, the processor may assist you in getting quotes for insurance based on the lender's requirements. This could be very helpful to meet minimum requirements for insurance coverage, and you can change insurers or level of coverage at a more convenient time.

YOUR RIGHTS AS A BUYER

The U.S. Department of Housing and Urban Development provides guidelines for all parties involved in the home buying process, drawn from a number of pertinent laws. These laws outline your rights as a buyer and designate appropriate agencies to administer their legal provisions. Such laws give you legal recourse should you suffer housing discrimination, be the victim of misrepresentation or otherwise be the victim of unfair practices with regard to home ownership.

The mortgage industry is subject to the actions of several regulatory bodies that determine the policies and procedures that govern the industry. Following is a list of the main agencies and their responsibilities:

Agency	Description
Federal Trade Commission	An independent administrative agency whose main function is enforcing the requirements of the Federal Credit Statutes that affect the Mortgage Banking Industry (Equal Credit Opportunity Act, Fair Credit Reporting Act, Fair Debt Collection Practices Act and Truth in Lending Act).
Federal Reserve Board	Issues regulations to implement the Truth in Lending Act and Equal Opportunity Credit Act.
Department of Housing and Urban Development	Originates departmental policies and publishes regulations to implement legislation passed by Congress. This department has authority over the National and Fair Housing Acts and the Real Estate Settlement Procedures Act (RESPA).
Federal Emergency Management Agency	Administers the National Flood Insurance Program through the Federal Insurance Administration.
Department of Veteran Affairs	Provides home loan opportunities for eligible veterans.

Fair Housing Act

This Act prohibits discrimination in the sale, rental, or financing of housing, and in the provision of brokerage services, based on race, color, religion, national origin, sex, handicap, or familial status. This act covers all segments of the real estate industry including brokers, builders, apartment owners, sellers, and mortgage lenders.

Fair Credit Reporting Act

Designed to ensure that consumer reporting agencies exercise fairness, confidentiality, and accuracy in preparing and disclosing credit information. This Act also limits the delivering of credit reports to those authorized to receive them but also allows consumers to acquire their own credit information from credit agencies and to dispute information that the consumers believe is wrong.

National Flood Insurance Act

Lenders must require flood insurance when the real estate property is the collateral and it is located in a flood zone, as shown in the appraisal. The Federal Emergency Management Agency (FEMA) issues regulations and guidelines under the authority of this law.

Truth in Lending Act (TILA)

TILA is found in Title I of the Consumer Credit Protection Act. Its purpose is to regulate the stated costs and terms of a loan. In general, it applies to any entity that offers credit for personal or household use. The credit offered must be subject to a finance charge and payable in more than four installments by written agreement.

Real Estate Settlement Procedures Act (RESPA)

The U.S. Department of Housing and Urban Development, through its Secretary, is authorized to issue regulations to implement the provisions of the Real Estate Settlement Procedures Act. RESPA is designed to provide homebuyers with a better understanding of the loan closing process or settlement of the loan closing costs. Under the provisions of the act, the lender is required to provide borrowers a booklet giving homebuyers detailed information on loan transaction settlement costs and procedures. RESPA also prohibits the payment of any fee, kickback, or similar payment for "referring a loan" or other real estate settlement business. Covered under this act are requirements related to disclosures to the borrower such as transfers of servicing, complaint resolutions and damages, costs, and transfers by lenders, among other industry practices. In addition, RESPA pertains to mortgage broker compensation by regulating fees received from lenders, not for referral of loans, but for services rendered. Brokers are required to perform services that are related to the fees they receive, sometimes referred to as a "yield spread premium" (YSP). The YSP, or rebate, is in the range of 1 percent to 4 percent and affects your interest rate.

Compensable services have three primary requirements related to the lender that must be satisfied to avoid violation of the Real Estate Settlements Procedures Act:

1. The lender's agent must take the application (loan officer).

2. The lender's agent must perform at least five additional items on a list of origination activities that is included in HUD's letter.

3. The fee for service must be reasonably related to the market value of the services that are performed.

Following is a list of services for which fees may be charged under the law:

1. Taking the information from the borrower and completing the application.

2. Analyzing the prospective borrower's income and debt and pre-qualifying him or her to determine the

maximum mortgage that the borrower can afford.

3. Educating the prospective borrower in the home buying and financing process, advising borrower about the different types of loan products available, and demonstrating how closing costs and monthly payments would vary under each product.

4. Collecting financial information (tax returns, bank statements) and other related documents that are part of the loan application process.

5. Providing disclosures (TIL, GFE, others) to the borrower.

6. Maintaining regular contact with the borrower, realtors, and lenders between the application and the closing period to let them know the status of the application and to get any additional information needed.

7. Assisting the borrower in understanding and clearing credit problems.

8. Requesting verification of employment or deposit.

9. Ordering appraisals.

10. Ordering inspections.

11. Ordering legal documents.

Brokers and lenders must issue both the Good Faith Estimate (GFE) and the Truth in Lending (TIL) statements within the first three days after receiving your loan application.

6

THE CREDIT REPORT

This chapter discusses the credit report, credit bureaus, companies that report credit, and tips and tools to improve a credit score before making a major purchase.

WHAT IS A CREDIT REPORT?

A credit report summarizes all your personal information such as your legal name, nicknames, or maiden names; your current and past residences; job history (if reported); date of birth; social security number; and most importantly, your debt history including authorized inquiries by creditors and a statistical measure of the risk in awarding you a loan.

According to the Fair Credit Reporting Act, you are entitled to one free credit report once a year (currently varies in some states) or within 90 days after you have been notified of a denial of credit, employment, or insurance due to your credit report.

Lenders and brokers get a Residential Mortgage Credit Report, also known as a Standard Factual Data Credit Report. In this report, all the information existing in the three major credit reporting agencies is consolidated into an easy-to-read format. A credit report is only valid for 90 days.

More will be explained about credit reports, but what if you have never used credit or have not been awarded conventional instruments of credit that would normally appear on a Residential Mortgage Credit Report? In this case, a nontraditional mortgage credit report (Alternative Credit) is compiled. The credit bureau will verify the applicant's non-traditional credit references, usually debts requiring periodic payments with intervals of no longer than three months. These accounts may include:

- Rental payments

- Utility bills

- Insurance payments

- Other rental payments (e.g., furniture, appliances)

- Medical bills

- School tuition

- Child care

- Private party accounts

Who Regulates Credit Reporting?

The Federal Trade Commission is the main agency that regulates credit, and the Bureau of Consumer Protection is the section that administrates and acts upon consumer complaints.

As mentioned above, the major pieces of legislation regarding credit are: the Fair Credit Reporting Act, the Equal Credit Opportunity Act, and the Fair Debt Collection Act. In the event that you believe the information contained in the credit bureau report to be false or inaccurate, you have the right to dispute those parts of the report and correct them.

The largest mortgage investors in the country, Fannie Mae and Freddie Mac, must approve credit-reporting services. These two companies require that for mortgage purposes the following information must be included in a Standard Factual Data Credit Report:

- Borrower's name, address, and length of residence (history of residency must cover a period of more than two years).

- Borrower's social security number.

- Verification of employment (minimum two-year history).

- Must list open or closed accounts, slow payments, collections from at least three different reporting agencies.

- Inquiries from lenders or creditors who have received requests for credit within the past 90 days.

- Public records, such as judgments, tax liens, and bankruptcies.

What is a Credit Bureau?

A credit reporting agency documents your financial behavior over the past seven years. It maintains and issues credit reports and files your financial activity in its database. The Fair Credit Reporting Act defines a credit bureau as "...any person, which, for monetary fees, dues, or on a cooperative nonprofit basis, regularly engages in whole or in part in the practice of assembling or evaluating consumer credit information or other information on consumers for the purpose of furnishing consumer reports to third parties, and which uses any means or facility of interstate commerce for the purpose of preparing or furnishing consumer reports."

The major credit reporting agencies are Equifax, Experian, and TransUnion.

IMPROVING YOUR CREDIT SCORE

Credit Score

Credit scores received a great deal of attention in 1995. Though credit scores had been used by the consumer credit and mortgage industries long before 1995, their use was not generally known and disclosure of the practice came as a shock to the general public.

Credit scores had been used in other types of consumer credit for more than 40 years, however. Fair Isaac and Company (FICO) in northern California developed a scoring system following World War II to fund purchases by returning soldiers who wanted to buy cars on credit. The scoring system predicted mathematically the likelihood of a consumer defaulting on a loan.

The system, since refined, applies a sophisticated mathematical model to credit behavior and, in part, bases your credit score on the statistical behavior of other borrowers like you.

A numerical score ranging from 300 to 900, with the low end of the scale indicating a poor credit risk, is calculated to tell a lender whether or not he should fund your home purchase. As an example, a credit score of 620 is stated as the cutoff point for issuing loans which are funded by Fannie Mae or Freddie Mac. If you are given a score below 620, you will be positioned in the private "sub-prime" market where interest rates are higher.

Factors That Build Credit Score

According to Fair Isaac and Company, the following items determine your credit risk score:

- 35 percent of the score is determined by payment histories on your credit accounts, with recent history weighed a bit more heavily than the ones in the past.

- 30 percent is based upon the amount of debt you have outstanding with all creditors (remaining balance to be paid).

- 15 percent is produced on the basis of how long you have been a credit user; a longer history is better if you have always made payments on time.

- 10 percent is contained by very recent history and how you have been actively seeking and getting credit in the past few months (authorized inquiries).

- 10 percent is calculated from the mix of credit you hold,

including installment loans, such as car loans, leases, mortgages, and credit cards, among others

The credit scores appearing in the Residential Mortgage Credit Report that your lender or broker receives will consolidate information from three of the following credit reporting agencies:

- Equifax

- Beacon

- TransUnion

- Empirica

- Experian

- FICO

Credit scores are developed by Fair Isaac and Company in cooperation with the three credit reporting agencies so the score cannot be altered by any of them. If you discover inaccurate information in any of the three credit reports that affects your credit score, you will have to initiate an investigation through the credit agency, but they will not delete any account or make changes to your information.

The higher the FICO credit score, the lower the risk of default. Both Fannie Mae and Freddie Mac define a FICO score above 620 as a demonstration of credit responsibility, and a high score of 660 or above may be used to offset a high debt-to-income ratio or other weakness in the loan application.

Both Fannie Mae and Freddie Mac caution lenders against

declining credit based solely on credit scores. Applicants with a perfect credit history and payment record but a credit score below 620 due to other reasons, like a limited credit history, are often declined credit unfairly or placed in the more expensive sub-prime market. In those cases, lenders are encouraged to obtain scores from each of the three major reporting agencies to compile a more complete credit history for the applicant. It is also recommended that the lenders use the middle score when they obtain three and the lower score if there are only two.

How credit scores are used in making the loan decision may be different depending on the borrower's situation and location. For example, in some cases, the primary borrower must make 60 percent or more of the total gross income when applying jointly or the lender will default to the lowest middle score of the borrowers' credit scores. The following table demonstrates this possibility.

Example 1: An individual applicant with the following credit scores:

Experian   685

Equifax   679

TransUnion   700

The lender will use the middle score of 685

Example 2: Co-borrowers, the primary borrower and another person (husband, wife, fiancé), the co-borrower, applying for a mortgage loan with credit scores as follows:

Borrower

Experian   685

Equifax   679

TransUnion 700

Co-borrower

Experian   654

Equifax   642

TransUnion 625

The primary borrower makes $5,000 a month and has a middle score of 685; the co-borrower makes $3,900 a month and a middle score of 642.

In this case, the primary borrower's income is only 56 percent of the total gross income ($5,000 divided by $8,900 = 56 percent) Consequently, the co-borrower's credit score of 642 will be used.

IMPROVING YOUR FICO SCORE

There may be little you can do to improve your score if you're buying a home now, but over time there several things you can do to improve your score in anticipation of large or unexpected expenditures, including the purchase of a new home.

- Handle your credit as wisely as you handle your money. Limit its use to what is prudent and to what demonstrates responsible use of credit. Generally, you should need only one or two consumer credit cards, and you should make charges on them that will be paid in full each month.

- Shopping around for credit can adversely affect your credit rating, particularly if done within a short period of time — less than a year. Insurance companies may also use credit information to determine your insurability and your insurance rates. Be careful when shopping for insurance that you do not request quotes from more than two or three insurers.

- Reduce, pay off, close, and consolidate your debt if you have high outstanding balances.

- Pay your bills on time. Late payments can be very damaging to your credit.

- Avoid offers of no payment for an extended period of time or payment on interest only, which might be reported to a credit reporting agency as the full amount owed including interest and will appear to exceed your credit limit when full payments begin.

- If you have a dispute with a creditor, pay the bill before taking legal action or place the amount in escrow. Otherwise, the creditor may report the balance as not paid or late.

FIXING YOUR CREDIT RATING

You and only you can improve your credit, but if you find yourself in over your head, get professional help immediately. You're not alone — bad things do happen to good people — and there are many professionals available to assist you. A consumer credit counseling agency is a good place to start, and they may recommend the services of an attorney and make referrals if your situation warrants it. There are also companies that offer services to repair your credit, but be wary; it makes little sense to go into debt to get rid of debt, and only you can repair your credit.

Every credit report includes up to four score factors that clarify why a credit score was low. The list of possibilites includes:

- Amount owed in accounts is too high.

- Delinquency on accounts.

- Too few bank revolving accounts.

- Too many bank accounts with balances.

- Consumer finance accounts.

- Account payment history too new to rate.

- Too many inquiries during the last 12 months.

- Too many accounts opened in last 12 months.

- Proportion of balances to credit limit is too high on bank revolving accounts or other revolving accounts.

- Amount owed on revolving account is too high.

- Length of revolving history is too short.

- Time since delinquency too recent or unknown.

- Length of credit history is too short.

- Lack of recent bank revolving account information.

- Lack of recent account information.

- No recent nonmortgage balance information.

- Number of accounts with delinquency.

- Too few accounts currently paid as agreed.

- Insufficient time since derogatory public record or collection.

- Amount past due on accounts.

- Serious delinquency, derogatory public record, or collection required.

- Too many bank or national revolving accounts with balances.

- No recent revolving balances.

- Proportion of loan balances to loan amounts is too high.

- Lack of recent loan information.

- Date of last inquiry too recent.

- Time since most recent account opening is too short.

- Number of revolving accounts.

- Number of retail accounts.

- Number of established accounts.

- No recent bankcard balances.

- Too few accounts with recent payment information.

- Payments due on accounts (for bankruptcy).

The most common credit issues reported in an individual's credit history are excessive debt, collections, bankruptcy, late payments, and public records (tax liens, judgments). It is worth the time to take a closer look at these problems.

- Excessive debt. The key word here is excessive. Credit scores do not necessarily reward the lack of debt, but they do reward your demonstrated ability to manage it. To reiterate the discussion above, pay off outstanding balances on credit cards every month. If the balance has gotten ahead of you, pay more than the minimum and reduce the balance below 50 percent of your limit as quickly as you can. If you have too many credit card accounts — one or two is enough — pay off one card at a time and add that card's payment to the payment of another card. Close the accounts when paid off.

- Collections. Unpaid or delinquent debts are often submitted to a collection agency for special handling. That action is reported to a credit reporting agency. Satisfying the debt is very important, of course, but even when resolved, there must be sufficient time between the date of resolution and the date of your application for a loan for it to affect your credit score. Never ignore an unpaid balance thinking there is little you can do. Contact your creditors and discuss why you are currently unable to make payment. They may offer alternative payment schedules or arrangements that will prevent the debt from being sent out for collection. They have every reason to do so because it means they can avoid the trouble and expense of collection, legal action, and so forth, and they would much rather receive some money than nothing at all. Be honest with them and work with them; you owe them that and more, but it will benefit you both.

- Public records. Actions you might take to resolve matters of public record depend greatly on the type of legal action that has been taken against you. If you wish to purchase a home, it may benefit you more to resolve a legal action previously contested than to further damage your credit rating by standing your ground. In other cases, it may be imperative that the issue be resolved; an IRS tax lien is a good case in point. Once a tax lien is satisfied, the IRS issues a certificate of release, which is registered by the county recorder and declares your debt to the IRS as paid or released. Be sure that's done before applying for a loan so lenders know the IRS no longer has cause to place a lien on the property for collateral against your debt to them.

- Keep in mind that the status of your credit accounts is reported by creditors to the reporting agencies once a month. It's important that you time your payoffs and other actions so that they appear on your credit report before you make application for a loan or your credit score will show little improvement.

If you are in the middle of the loan process and need to improve your score, there is something you can do in cooperation with the bank, credit union, or broker handling your loan application. The procedure is called "rapid rescore" and is used to update credit information quickly in your credit report. If you have already paid off a credit card balance, for example, but the credit report was issued at the beginning of the monthly reporting period and does not include that transaction in the report received by the lender later in the month, you can initiate a rapid rescore to get the report updated.

- Request from the creditor a letter showing you have made payment and have a zero balance.

- Request of the lender that they submit the letter to the agency providing them with a consolidated mortgage credit report for forwarding to the three major credit reporting agencies (Experian, Equifax, and TransUnion).

Once processed and fees ascertained, the lender's reporting agency will submit the documentation to the three agencies who will update the information.

Updating collection information can be done similarly.

- Indicate to your creditors your willingness to pay off the collection amount, but request that they update the account information using the Universal Data Form.

- Make full payment.

- The account information will be reported to the three credit reporting agencies in the Universal Data Form as "paid" rather than as "collection paid." Consequently, your credit score will not factor how recently the debt was paid.

WHAT LENDERS LOOK AT IN YOUR CREDIT REPORT

The credit report and the credit score are a fundamental part in making lending decisions, but remember that a credit reporting agency is a third party in the transaction, and it only reports and updates information as required by law. It cannot, therefore, give an opinion regarding your credit worthiness. That is the role and responsibility of a mortgage lender and its underwriters. In this section, we examine their possible criteria, which varies from lender to lender.

WHY CREDIT SCORING IS IMPORTANT

The largest mortgage investors in the United States, Fannie Mae and Freddie Mac, issued letters to the mortgage industry in 1995 in which they stated their approval of the use of credit scores for evaluating credit risk. In those letters, they encouraged lenders to take advantage of the efficiency and consistency credit scores offer, saying:

Credit scores should be used as part of a careful, comprehensive analysis of the unique characteristics of each individual mortgage application.

Credit scoring allows lenders to:

- Give objective and consistent assessments so the borrower is offered the loan program that is most suitable.

- Remove the potential for unfairness and comply with fair lending laws.

- Offer more favorable terms to those who demonstrate the ability to manage debt.

- Control delinquencies and charge offs.

- Speed up the decision-making process, thereby allowing the underwriter to focus on more complex decisions.

- Make their underwriting criteria more flexible, accept more loan applications, and avoid poor-performing loans.

What can you expect when you do not have a good credit history? In the mortgage lending industry, just as in other lending industries, an individual's credit is broken down into four categories:

- Collateral – security for the repayment of the loan; in the mortgage lending industry, the house is collateral.

- Capacity – the ability to repay the loan, focusing mainly on employment and income.

- Character – the importance you associate with using credit; how much debt you have and how much credit you ask for routinely.

- Credit – a demonstrated ability to manage debt; how you have been using and paying your debt; for how long you have had credit; if you've had late payments, collections, derogatory accounts, bankruptcy, judgments, or liens.

If a lender, in considering these three general criteria, raises specific questions regarding your credit history and resulting credit score, you will have to address their concerns specifically.

Slow Payments

You will have to explain in writing the reasons you were slow to make payments on any account, including those payments currently late. Be prepared to provide evidence that payments have been brought up to date.

Judgments, Charge-off, Collections, Garnishments, and Tax Liens

Again, be prepared to show written evidence, including pertinent legal documentation, that legal actions against you have been satisfied or will not complicate the status of the property, the loan, or its repayment.

Bankruptcy

If you have a bankruptcy in your credit history, you may still be considered for a loan. However, you will have to provide the following documentation.

- A written explanation to support the reason or reasons for bankruptcy and evidence of your attempt to reinstate credit since the bankruptcy.

- A copy of the bankruptcy petition to include the schedule of debts.

- The final discharge of bankruptcy showing the schedule of debts discharged.

Some lenders who specialize in loans to individuals with credit problems will fund your purchase if there is a bankruptcy in your credit history but at a much higher interest rate, while others will require that the bankruptcy must have occurred more than a designated number of years prior to the loan application. There are different categories of bankruptcy, and the waiting period for each type of bankruptcy will vary from lender to lender, though the standard is as follows:

- **Chapter 7** – Individual renounces his or her debts, then a liquidation proceeding occurs in which a trustee is appointed or elected to collect the debtor's nonexempt assets, sell them, and distribute the proceeds, if any, to unsecured creditors. Waiting period is four years from the date of discharge.

- **Chapter 11** – This kind of bankruptcy occurs when there is a reorganization of business, in which the business proposes a plan of payments to creditors. Earnings from the reorganized business are used to make payments. The debtor usually keeps all assets.

- **Chapter 13** – This applies to a wage earner, where he or she establishes a plan of repayment to creditors from his or her future income. Usually payments are made to creditors through a trustee who handles payments toward the amount allocated when the individual files for bankruptcy. Payments become due after the wage earner files under Chapter 13 and are made directly by the debtor to creditors. Lenders could ask for a four-year waiting period from the date of the original petition.

In the cases of both Chapter 7 and Chapter 13, the individual who filed should demonstrate a good faith effort to repay debts. Two years after the bankruptcies have been discharged, the borrowers must establish at least three new accounts, preferably installment debts such as car loans, and all three new established accounts must be kept current.

It is also important to note that in April 2005, the Bankruptcy Abuse Prevention and Consumer Protection act of 2005 was signed by President George W. Bush and became effective for cases filed on or after October 2005. This Act makes changes to consumer bankruptcy that may affect those who have or will file for bankruptcy and plan to purchase a home. More information and be found on this law at the U.S. Bankruptcy Court website.

Inquiries

If your credit report shows an excessive number of inquiries in the previous year, you must provide an explanation as to the purpose of each inquiry and disclose if they resulted in a new credit account and current outstanding balance, which must be verified. For mortgage loan purposes, credit inquiries are verified for the 90 days prior to your application for a mortgage loan.

PERIOD OF RECORD

Entries on your credit record will remain for specific periods of time. The fact that these records still appear on your credit record does not mean you are ineligible for a home loan.

- **Bankruptcies** – 10 years from date of petition, dismissal, or discharge, depending on the chapter filed.

- **Tax liens** – 7 years from date of payment.

- **Judgments** – 7 years from date of entry.

- **Notices of default** – 10 years from date of entry.

- **Collections** – 7 years from date of last activity.

- **Repossessions** – 10 years from date of last activity.

CONSUMER CREDIT COUNSELING PLANS

Consumer credit counseling services (CCCS) assist individuals with financial management of debts in an attempt to avoid further delinquencies or possible bankruptcy. Generally, creditors agree to receive a lesser repayment under a Consumer Credit Counseling Plan. This kind of plan appears in your credit report, or it may be discovered later if you do not disclose that information in your loan application.

The features or conditions of this program could include:

- Review of satisfactory payment history for up to 24 months.

- A lender may require the plan and require payment for the plan at closing.

- A higher interest rate on the mortgage may be assessed.

YOUR ASSETS AND SAVINGS

Assets and savings can be a determining factor for lenders who might fund your loan even if there are credit problems. You will submit records of your assets and savings with your loan application by filling in the "Assets and Liabilities" section. The information provided must be supported by documentation demonstrating that you have sufficient funds to complete the loan transaction. In addition, you may be required to show evidence of liquid assets and savings to ensure you have the necessary funds to make mortgage payments. The documentation required depends on the type of loan and will be determined by a number of factors, including the documentation type[17], loan to value (LTV) or combined loan to value (CLTV) ratio, as well as your profile and credit score.

Assets generally used to support your loan application may include but are not limited to:

- Money in a checking, saving, money market, certificate of deposit, or individual retirement account (IRA).

- Earnest money deposit.

- Stocks and other securities.

- Bonds.

- Sale of assets such as automobile or boat.

- 401(k) retirement plans.

- Mutual funds.

[17]More information in documentation type will be provided in chapter 7.

- Life insurance cash value.

- Municipal grants.

- Relocation credits and residence liquidation.

- Tax refunds.

- Gift funds.

- Contributions by interested parties, such as seller, builder, developer, real estate agent, and mortgage broker.

Assets listed should be liquid funds that can easily be converted to available funds in a timely manner.

The following example demonstrates many of the exigencies of the loan process as discussed:

A woman relocating to Las Vegas hoped to purchase a new home even though her credit history reflected a bankruptcy only two years prior. Her income, though very good, was not enough to build savings because the cost of living in Las Vegas was quite high. She decided to explore the possibility of purchasing a home anyway and elected to use the balance of her 401(k) retirement plan as a listed asset. She was able to secure 100 percent financing (split in two loans, 80/20 percent) for $435,000, the sales price for a newly built house in a very nice gated community. The builder gave her 3 percent of the sales price for closing costs, equaling an amount of $13,050. With the help of a mortgage broker who shopped around for the best loan for her specific situation and credit score (her middle credit score was 611 at the time of her loan application), a lender funded her purchase under the following loan program:

- One loan of 80 percent of the house value; adjustable-rate mortgage with a 7.99 percent interest rate for 30 years.

- Second loan of 20 percent of the house value; fixed-rate mortgage with an 11.5 percent interest rate for 30 years due in 15 (called a "balloon payment").

The lender verified her employment history (2 years), her rent for her previous residences (2 years), and information on her provided 401(k) statements, which she used to prove she had reserves for three months of mortgage payments.

The final loan figures are better represented below:

ITEM	AMOUNT
Monthly payment for 1st loan (principal and interest) based on 80 percent of the house sales price $ 348,000.00	$ 2,551.08
Monthly payment for 2nd loan (principal and interest) based on 20 percent of the house sales price $ 87,000.00	$ 861.55
Closing costs: Mortgage loan origination for 1st loan (1 point)	$ 3,480.00
Mortgage loan origination for 2nd loan (1 point)	$ 870.00
Processing fees	$ 700.00
Lender's fees	$ 1,400.00
Title and recording fees	$ 2,760.00
Total closing costs	$ 9,210.00
Earnest money deposit	$ 2,000.00

At the closing of escrow, and after her loan was funded, she received reimbursement of $3,840.00.

Lenders have restrictions and guidelines when it comes to the use of concessions on the part of sellers, builders, and others involved in the deal and with regard to assets that are listed to prove liquidity. Among sources of funds often found unacceptable are:

- Money obtained from a personal or unsecured loan, such as cash in advance on a revolving charge account or an unsecured line of credit.

- A gift that must be repaid (even partially).

- Material furnished by the borrower that is not part of a pre-closing agreement with the builder.

- Any payment received from participating in the sale transaction, such as real estate commission payments.

- Borrowed funds not secured by an asset.

- Cash-on-hand that cannot be verified back to its original source.

- Funds derived from Public Employees Retirement System (PERS) plans are commonly not accepted by lenders because the applicant cannot borrow against the fund at any time; these accounts usually can be liquidated only upon retirement or death.

Concessions for closing costs have a limit that could range from 3 percent 6 percent depending on the loan-to-value or combined-loan-to-value, meaning the percentage may not exceed:

- 3 percent of the lesser of the sale price or appraised value if the loan-to-value or combined-loan-to-value ratio is greater than 90 percent and the property will be occupied as a primary residence.

- 6 percent of the lesser of the sale price or appraised value if the mortgage is secured by a primary residence and the LTV or CLTV ratio is 90 percent or less.

The lender may also ask for what's called "sourcing" and "seasoning" of your assets, depending on the loan program for which you qualify and it requirements.

Sourcing

Sourcing refers to tracking funds to their original source, and the source must be acceptable to the lender. If funds are derived from nonliquid sources, for example, the sale of assets, they are not required to be seasoned, which is to say they do not have to be in a borrower's account for any length of time.

Seasoning

A lender may require seasoning of funds required for closing costs and reserves if they are derived from liquid assets (e.g., bank accounts, including certificates of deposit, savings, checking accounts, and IRAs). Funds are considered seasoned if they have been in your account for a required period of time, generally 60 days prior to the closing of the loan, but if the funds have not been in your account for the required period, you must provide documentation verifying the source from which the funds originated.

Normally if you are a first-time homebuyer, a lender will not require verification of your funds if you qualify for a program that lists your employment and income information as sufficient to secure the loan.

An Example of Creative Financing

A woman who had moved from Mexico to Florida and had been working for only a year subsequent to the issuance of a work permit and permanent resident alien card applied for a home loan. She qualified as a first-time home buyer but required verification on previous employment because it was abroad and verification of her current employment and income for one year. She stated on her loan application (Form 1003) that she had savings of $8,500, but the lender did not ask for written verification of these funds. Her current monthly income was $3,360.

She was awarded a loan package of $240,000 split between two loans. The first loan was for 75 percent of the price of the house ($180,000) and was an adjustable rate mortgage for a term of 45 years with a fixed rate of 6.875 percent for the first five years. The monthly payment of principal and interest totaled $1080.67. The second loan was for 25 percent of the price of the house ($60,000) and was a fixed-rate mortgage with a term of 45 years but due in 30 years. It carried an interest rate of 9.75 percent and a monthly payment of $493.75.

The Debt-to-Income-Ratio (DTI) was a deciding factor for these loans. Adding the two monthly payments and her current minimum payment for credit cards of $100 per month, her total debt, including mortgage payments, was $1,674.42, or a DTI of exactly 50 percent, a ratio acceptable to her lender under these terms.

The example demonstrates some of the conditions that might allow you to buy a house with zero percent down and no closing costs out-of-pocket.

A Real Estate Agent can offer a first-time homebuyer representation, advice, and support throughout the often complex process of a real estate transaction. First-time homebuyers are often not aware of the many elements involved in purchasing a new home. I call it having "All Your Ducks in a Row." If you don't have certain things in place when you go into negotiations for a house, it makes the situation even more complex. If those elements are not in place, chances are you will lose the property to someone who has those things in place. What first-time homebuyers don't realize is that it does not cost them anything to have this representation. The seller typically pays the agent fees.

Personally, I will not work with buyers if they do not have that pre-qualification in place. First, it's one of the major ducks in that row of things you need to have in line to give yourself the best chance of winning a bid in a competitive marketplace. Second, when first-time homebuyers start out, they don't really have a clear idea of what they can afford. More times than not they have either overestimated or underestimated what they can afford. The pre-qualification process allows them to get down to the actual amount that they can afford, making everyone feel more at ease.

I think the most common mistake first-time homebuyers make is they don't look at the bigger picture, and they become too emotional about the process. There is a certain level of flexibility that one has to have to understand that you are not going to get everything you want in your first home purchase. If you get hung up on the small stuff and allow yourself to worry about the sacrifices that may be called upon you to make, you will never get through the process. There will always be a million and one reasons to back out to the deal. Giving into fear and lacking in the confidence it takes to know that you can "do this" is the biggest mistake first-time homebuyers make.

I have working relationships with mortgage lenders, bankers, and real estate attorneys. I need to be able to pick up the phone or e-mail a contact if my client does not have that particular association in place. In New York City, a buyer-agent relationship written agreement is a rare occurrence. It is usually a verbal agreement.

First-time home buyers generally want to purchase a condo or a co-op. If they are going to buy a house, they tend to want something that has an additional unit in order to generate income to offset expenses. Two to three-families residences are in high demand.

The average market value of a single family residence in New York really varies. However, on the low end you are talking $600,000 to one million plus. Obviously, in New York City, you can see things on the high-end at 10 million plus. It really all depends on the location and the specification of what you are looking for.

I have so many stories about successful closings. But to be quite honest, there is not much difference between the purchase transactions that fall apart and the ones that go on to successful completion. It really all comes down to how much a buyer wants the home, or how motivated a seller is to sell the home. No matter what the buyer's situation, where there is a will there is a way. If you are willing to do what it takes to put all the players into place to make the purchase of your home, you can do it. If there is no will, there is no way that they will be successful at seeing the transaction through. There are a million and one reasons to not move forward. Most of these reasons are rooted in fear. You have to be fearless.

I find that no matter how much you explain the process the customer is always going to have questions. Constant communication has to take place to make the customers feel comfortable that they are well informed. But I sometimes find myself explaining the same element of the process a million and one different ways. That is when I have to be patient, understanding and open to ease their minds. If I don't know the answer to a customer's question, you can rest assured that I know someone who does know the answer to the question. I am not afraid to say, "I will get back to you on that issue."

Only rarely do I negotiate, so the seller pays the buyer's closing costs. However, I would never say never. I have learned in this business it's all about negotiation. If you don't ask, you won't receive. If you ask, you just might find that people would be willing to do the most outrageous things to get the deal done. It really all depends on the motivation of all relevant parties. So it doesn't hurt to ask for something outrageous—the shock doesn't come from being denied your outrageous request because sometimes you are shocked when your request is granted.

I have been in the business for two years. I got into it for the freedom to dictate my own work schedule and to have more control over what I do with my time and energy. I love the idea of picking and choosing which clients to work with. I love the idea that every day is different, and my calendar is filled with appointments that I make or break. I am an independent contractor, so I work for myself. It is very difficult at times managing time and sticking to productivity goals, but it is a very satisfying feeling to persevere in a field in which many others fail.

Jason Hunter
Irvine Realty Group, Inc.
122 East 55th Street, Third Floor
New York, New York 10022
Telephone (212) 754-7100 Ext. 104
Facsimile (212) 754-7937
Cellular (347) 277-6791
Email: Jason@irvinegroup.com
www.irvinegroup.com

Mortgage investors play an important role in the home buying process.

7

WHERE TO FIND
THE BEST FINANCING

This chapter may prove to be the most interesting in this handbook because it introduces you to the mortgage banking industry, the important role mortgage investors play in the home buying process, the lending institutions that make up the industry, the titles and job profiles of the people who grant loans, the finance packages that are offered by the industry, and the types of loans that are available to you and other home buyers. You will also be introduced to some strategies for home buyers such as being pre-qualified before signing a purchase contract and using IRAs to cover certain expenses. Both FHA and VA loans will be explained as well.

THE SYSTEM

The two major mortgage investors in the United States have been mentioned throughout this book, but in this section, it will be explained more specifically who these companies are and the role they play in the mortgage industry.

- **Government National Mortgage Association** (Ginnie Mae) — An offshoot of Fannie Mae created in 1968 by the federal government to purchase government-backed loans. This private company buys FHA and VA loans with the full faith and credit of the U.S. Treasury backing all of their loans, making these loans among the safest investments possible.

- **Federal National Mortgage Association** (Fannie Mae) — This company was first started by the federal government in 1938 to provide supplementary assistance to the secondary market for residential mortgages by supplying a degree of liquidity for mortgage investments, thereby improving the distribution of investment capital available for residential mortgage financing. Fannie Mae purchases FHA, VA, and conventional loans (95 percent of the loans purchased). Fannie Mae is a private company with stockholders; the Treasury of the United States holds a substantial amount of the stock.

- **Federal Home Loan Mortgage Corporation** (Freddie Mac) — This is a federally charted corporation, created to provide a secondary market for loans originated through savings and loans and commercial banks, and operating similarly to Fannie Mae.

- **Private Jumbo** – These entities have grown larger and more important since the mid-80s. They provide a source of funds for jumbo loans (over the lending limits of Fannie Mae and Freddie Mac), but most of the companies use Fannie Mae and Freddie Mac guidelines as a reference for underwriting though they may also have their own special guidelines.

Both Fannie Mae and Freddie Mac define their underwriting guidelines by using three specific criteria:

1. The property has sufficient collateral/security for the requested loan. This is the reason an appraisal is needed by lenders to ensure they are funding a property that is worth the sales price.

2. The borrower has the ability to repay the loan using verification of income and employment.

3. The borrower is willing to repay the loan through the borrower's credit worthiness.

The Mortgage Lending Industry is graphed in the following chart:

BORROWER

LOAN ORIGINATOR
(Bank, Credit Union, Wholesale Lender or Mortgage Broker)

LOAN PROCESSOR
(Bank, Credit Union, Wholesale Lender or Mortgage Broker)

LOAN UNDERWRITER
(Bank, Credit Union, Wholesale Lender)

FUNDER/CLOSER
(Bank, Credit Union, Wholesale Lender or Mortgage Broker)

INSURER/SHIPPER
(Bank, Credit Union, Wholesale Lender or Mortgage Broker)

SERVICING
(Servicing Company, Mortgage Banker or Portfolio)

SECONDARY MARKET
(Fannie Mae, Freddie Mac, Ginnie Mae or Private Conduit)

SOURCE OF MONEY
(Wall Street, Insurance Co, Bank, Portfolio, Pension Fund, Mutual Fund or Individual)

Job Titles and Duties

- **Loan Originator.** This is the person who starts the loan process, compiles relevant information provided by you and others, and acts as the conduit between you and the underwriter. A loan originator could be a loan officer, loan representative, loan consultant, loan broker, area manager, account executive, or loan originator.

- **Loan Processor.** The person who reviews, verifies, and processes all the paperwork for the loan package. The processor orders and evaluates the home appraisal; reviews the purchase agreement, the credit report, and all verifications; and deals with the escrow officer or lawyer, appraiser, credit bureau, real estate agents, title company, and underwriter. The loan processor also submits the loan package to the underwriter for approval.

- **Underwriter.** This is the person who approves or disapproves the loan package; he or she makes the decision as to whether the loan is sellable and insurable.

- **Funder/Closer.** The person who draws the final loan documents, makes sure all paperwork is complete, and authorizes the writing of funds into settlement.

Credit Grades

The different credit grades that may be assigned to a borrower, depending on his or her credit history and credit score are A+, A-, B, B-, C and D; these grades affect the interest rate and qualifying conditions for a borrower.

- **"A" loans** - A borrower can qualify for an "A" paper loan when he or she has good income, acceptable credit, a verifiable down payment and a property that appraises for the full value of its sales price. For lenders, an A loan is preferable because it can be closed fast and is readily sold in the secondary market.

- **"B" loans** – This kind of loan applies to a borrower who has a credit history of one or two late payments and high debt, therefore resulting in a loan that is harder to process and the borrower may get a higher interest rate.

- **"C" loans** – The borrower has poor credit, little income, many collections and in some cases bankruptcy.

- **"D" loans** – An applicant with very bad credit history, late payments, collections, bankruptcy, judgments, and some other credit issues. When loans are given to such borrowers, they usually have very high interest rates.

Approval of a loan often depends on how much people with bad credit are willing to pay for a loan; the greater the risk for the lender, the greater the interest they will charge.

Types of Loans

There are literally thousands of loan programs available in the mortgage industry as every lender tries to develop different programs to satisfy a special market niche. It would be impossible to review every type of loan, so only the main types will be discussed in this section. Most loan programs are just variations of the mortgage loans briefly outlined here.

Characteristics	FHA	VA	Conventional
Guaranteed or financed by	Government	Government	Private
Guidelines	Conforming	Conforming	• Conforming • Nonconforming Jumbo • Alt-A • Sub-prime
Type of documentation	Full documentation (pay-stubs, W-2, two years employment, two years residence history).	Full documentation (pay-stubs, W-2, etc)	Many
Max loan amount	$269,000 (1 unit)	$359,650	For conforming $410,000[18] Nonconforming (Jumbo) unlimited depending on the lender.
Credit grade	Non-Credit score	Non-Credit score	Credit score
Alternative credit	Must pay collections, tax liens, judgments, others.	Must pay collections, tax liens, judgments, others.	Most not to be paid, usually if they are below $5,000 in the case of collections, tax liens to be paid before or at closing. Depends on lender's guidelines.

[18]As of Dec. 2005, limits are updated constantly.

Bankruptcy	Borrower to wait four years after case is discharged.	Borrower to wait four years after case is discharged.	For conforming, two years after discharged; sub-prime, some lenders have programs in which accept BK from one day after discharged or petitioned.
Late in payments	Needs letter of explanation.	Needs letter of explanation.	For conforming, needs letter of explanation. No explanations needed for sub-prime.
Gifted funds for down payment or closing costs	Allowed but have to be sourced (tracked back to the source).	Allowed but have to be sourced (tracked back to the source).	For conforming is also allowed but has to be sourced; most lenders only allow using half of the gifted amount.
Down payment	3 percent	0 percent	From 0 percent, with subordinate financing[19]
Concessions for closing costs	Up to 6 percent for closing costs.	Up to 6 percent for closing costs and down payment.	Depending on the lender could be up to 6 percent for closing costs (recurring and non-recurring[20]).
Mortgage Insurance Premium upfront	Yes, and it is usually 1.5 percent of the loan amount.	None	None

[19]See glossary in Appendix B and Chapter 8.

[20]Definition for recurring and non-recurring closing costs are in chapter 8.

Mortgage insurance premium monthly	0.5 percent of total loan amount (loan amount + MIP upfront = total loan amount).	None	None
Funding fee	No	Calculated based upon the loan amount and whether the Veteran is a first-time or subsequent user. For a purchase, the VA funding fee ranges from 1.25 percent to 3.30 percent based upon the loan amount.	No
Private Mortgage Insurance	No	No	For conforming loans, borrower will have to pay mortgage insurance on a monthly basis if the down payment is less than 20 percent of the house sales price. For sub-prime, depending on the lender's guidelines.
Impounded	Yes	Yes	Depends on the lender's guidelines.

DTI Ratio	Up to 50 percent with excellent contributing factors such as savings, good alternative credit history, etc.	Up to 50 percent with excellent contributing factors, such as savings, good alternative credit history, etc.	Conforming and non-conforming: 40 percent to 45 percent. Sub-prime: 45 percent to 55 percent.
Loan programs	Fixed Rate Mortgage and Adjustable Rate Mortgage.	Fixed Rate Mortgage and Adjustable Rate Mortgage.	Fixed, ARM, Balloon, Interest Only, 40 and 45 yrs amortization, Home Equity Line of Credit.
Occupancy	Owner occupied, nonowner occupied.	Owner occupied, nonowner occupied.	Owner occupied, nonowner occupied (investment), second home, foreign national.
Interest paid in advance	From first day of the month.	From first day of the month.	Per day, starting on closing of escrow and to the end of the month.
Pest inspections	Require all and is mandatory.	Require all and is mandatory.	Not mandatory, lenders may ask for pest inspection but it can be waived by buyer.
Loan to Value	97 percent	100 percent	Up to 107 percent
Approved appraisers	Approved by FHA	Approved by VA	Not necessary

FHA and VA financing will be discussed later. Here we'll focus on conventional financing.

Conventional financing consists of conforming loans following Fannie Mae and Freddie Mac guidelines, jumbo loans, sub-prime (non-conforming), home equity loans, graduated payment mortgages, growing equity mortgages, reverse mortgages, balloon mortgages, and combination loans. Note that a conventional mortgage is a non-government loan financed with a value less than or equal to a specific amount established each year by major secondary lenders.

Conforming Loans

These kinds of loans meet all guidelines issued by Fannie Mae and Freddie Mac. The most important of these guidelines are:

- The buyer must be a legal U.S. resident (U.S. born or U.S. permanent resident alien with work permit).

- The buyer must purchase a house with the intention of using it as primary residence.

- The maximum loan amount as of December 2005 is $400,000 for one unit.

- The term of the loan is generally 30 years amortization, but 15- and 20-year terms are also offered.

Mortgage loans with a loan-to-value ratio over 80 percent require private mortgage insurance (PMI). Private mortgage insurance is issued to protect the lender against the borrower's default. It is issued by private mortgage insurance companies, and it is paid by the borrower on a monthly basis; PMI is added to a mortgage loan monthly payment, along with taxes and hazard insurance (impounds) if required by the lender.

The loan-to-value ratio is calculated by dividing the loan amount by the lesser of the sales price or appraised value; i.e. if you have a loan amount of $160,000 and the sales price or appraised value of the house is $200,000, your LTV ratio is 80 percent. In this example, the down payment would be 20 percent of the sales price or appraised value.

Jumbo Loans

These loans exceed the maximum limit allowed for conforming loans; even when these loans are financed by private investors and large financial institutions, lenders use Fannie Mae and Freddie Mac guidelines.

Nonconforming Loans

Today there is a huge market for nonconforming loans (also known as sub-prime). Borrowers who fall into this category do not meet the criteria set for Fannie Mae and Freddie Mac loans.

People who have higher debt ratios or poor credit or who have a recent bankruptcy are good candidates for these programs.

Home Equity Loans

This kind of loan is very interesting because real estate has traditionally been considered a non-liquid asset and as such can be converted to cash only by either selling or refinancing it. However, a home equity loan or home equity line of credit (HELOC) works very much like a consumer loan except the credit is limited to a percent of the borrower's equity on the house.

The principal feature of a HELOC is that it is usually placed in a second lien position (a second mortgage) after the original mortgage and at a higher interest rate. Recently, qualification for HELOC loans has become more difficult because state governments have issued new regulations to prevent consumers from falling prey to predatory lending practices. Under the terms of a HELOC, the borrower has access to a certain amount of money through a credit line that is equal to the amount of equity for the property.

Graduated Payment Mortgage

This loan is for borrowers who expect their income to increase in the future. The salient feature of this loan is an interest that is lower than the market rate making it easier for a borrower to qualify for a larger loan. Nevertheless, there is a risk involved in that borrowers assume they will have enough income to afford raised payments in the future. This is similar to an adjustable rate mortgage, but the rate increases at a set rate unlike an adjustable rate that fluctuates with the market.

Growing Equity Mortgage

In the early 80s the Growing Equity Mortgage (GEM) was developed as an alternative to creative financing. This loan is amortized like a conventional loan but using a repayment method that saves interest expense by 50 percent or more. The monthly payment can be increased up to double its original amount at the discretion of the borrower; additional amounts paid are dedicated to the principal balance rather than the interest. In this way, a mortgage loan with a longer term can be paid off in as little as 15 years and will save thousands of dollars in interest charges.

Reverse Mortgages

These mortgages are designed especially for elderly people with equity in their homes but limited cash; they allow individuals to retain homeownership while providing needed cash flow.

Having a reverse mortgage, the homeowner receives a specified amount every month for a specific term. The payments are drawn against the homeowner's equity in the home, and at the end on this term the borrower owes the lender the total amount that he or she received during the term plus interest.

Balloon Mortgage

This is a loan that comes due and payable before it is fully amortized. Today balloon mortgages are offered by sub-prime lenders, usually for second loans as subordinated financing of a primary loan. They are amortized over a period of 30 years, generally, but become due and payable after 15 years, which means the final payment may be huge. Consequently, it may be imprudent to wait the full 15 years to pay down the loan; usually these loans are refinanced after the pre-payment period is over.

Combination Loan

Combination loans were introduced in the final section of Chapter 6. By simultaneously combining a first and second mortgage at varying rates and terms, they allow the borrower a smaller down payment (even 0 percent) while avoiding having to pay private mortgage insurance. The most popular combinations are 80/10/10 (80 percent first loan, 10 percent second loan and 10 percent down payment); 80/20 (80 percent first loan, 20 percent second loan and 0 percent down payment), and most recently, 75/25 because the loan-to-value ratio for the first loan is lower, making it easier for the borrower to qualify, and the monthly payment is lower, as well, because the loan is calculated using a lower interest rate. Generally, the terms of the second loan are more severe, however, and the borrower must pay both loans simultaneously.

Interest Rates

While the loan types discussed in the previous section focus primarily on the methods of payment, the loans discussed in this section focus largely on the method of determining interest rates. In truth, the more traditional structure of the loans discussed here may be found among those previously discussed, but it is important to understand the distinctions.

Fixed-Rate Mortgages

With a Fixed-Rate Mortgage, the interest rate and monthly payment (principal and interest) will stay the same for the term of the loan. The most common terms are 30, 20 and 15 years, but lately some lenders have been introducing a 40 and 45-year term in order to qualify those borrowers who can better afford the lower resulting payment. The interest rate for this mortgage is generally higher.

Adjustable Rate Mortgages

With this loan, the interest rate will fluctuate based upon changes in the rate-index the loan is tied to; the most common indexes are 30-year U.S. Treasury Bills and the London Interbank Offering Rate (LIOR). The initial interest rate stays fixed for a set period, which ranges from one to seven years and is usually lower than conventional fixed rates. The advantage of this type of loan is that the borrower can usually afford a larger loan at the outset, which is an attractive option if there are no plans to remain in the house for a long period of time, if income is expected to rise later, or if initial repairs and renovations need to be done on the home that would otherwise use up extra savings or income.

The lender must provide an explanation of what index is being used to determine the interest rates and how the monthly payment will change based upon each newly adjusted interest rate. In addition, there must be a ceiling on the amount an interest rate can change over the life of the loan; Fannie Mae and Freddie Mac put a limit of +6 percent over the initial rate.

Interest Only Mortgages (IO)

An IO mortgage can be either a fixed rate or adjustable rate mortgage. The advantage of this loan is easier qualification for a loan because the monthly payment is for the interest only over a term of 5, 7, or even 10 years. After the initial period, however, the borrower will begin to pay principal and interest, making the monthly payment higher considerably higher than it would be in a conventional loan with consistent payments.

Buy-Down Mortgage

This loan is an option for those borrowers who do not qualify for a lower interest rate due to their debt-to-income ratio. To get a lower rate, the borrower pays additional points to reduce the interest rate for the first years. Because buy-down mortgages are usually in combination with an adjustable rate mortgage with an initial fixed rate for 2, 3, 5, or 7 years, the lowered rate will apply to the fixed period.

The following chart is provided to demonstrate the differences between loan types using a specific scenario:

Sales price $ 200,000	Borrower monthly income: $3,200
Down payment of 20 percent=$40,000	Monthly debt: $100
Loan amount $ 160,000	

Loan Feature	Fixed Rate	ARM	Interest Only	Buy-Down
Interest rate	7.25 percent	6.875 percent	7.00 percent	6.00 percent
Term	30 yrs	30 yrs	30 yrs	30 yrs
Standard rate or fully indexed rate		7.65 percent	7.65 percent	6.875 percent ARM, 7.65 percent
Buy-down points 0.875 percent				$1,400
Monthly payment principal and interest (five first yrs only for ARM, IO, and buy-down)	$1,091.48	$1,051.09	$933.33	$959.28
Monthly payment after first five years	$1,091.48	$1,135.22	$1,135.22	$1,135.22
Hazard insurance and taxes	$197	$197	$197	$197
Total debt (PITI[21] plus monthly debt)	$1,388.48	$1,348.09	$1,230.33	$1,256.28
DTI Ratio	43 percent	42 percent	38 percent	39 percent

[21]Principal, Interest, Taxes and Insurance

For the adjustable rate mortgage, the index is the LIBOR six-month rate, 4.65 percent, plus the lender margin of 3 percent for a total of 7.65 percent; this is called the fully indexed rate.

For interest only, the monthly payment is calculated multiplying the loan amount of $160,000 by the interest rate of 7 percent, then dividing the result by 12 to get the monthly payment. After the five-year interest-only period, the payment includes principal and interest. Most lenders require a minimum credit score to qualify for IO programs.

For buy-down, the points refer to the amount you would have to pay up front at close of escrow to buy down the interest rate (loan amount $160,000 x 0.875 percent= $1,400).

Debt-To-Income Ratio

This is a percentage of housing and monthly debts versus gross income. The DTI ratio is calculated by dividing the proposed housing and monthly debts by the gross income. Using the example above with the fixed rate monthly payment plus taxes, insurance, and other debt ($1,388.48 / $3,200), the resulting ratio is 43 percent of the borrower's gross income.

Mortgage guidelines refer to the front ratio as the percentage of proposed housing expense (PITI) divided by gross income, and to the back ratio as the percentage of proposed housing expense plus all monthly debt and obligations divided by gross income. The back ratio is the percentage used by lenders to qualify a borrower for a specific loan program.

Mortgage Brokers

A broker is an individual or company who shops around among many sources of funding, including mortgage banks, commercial banks, wholesale lenders, and others to find an interested lender with a loan program most suitable for the borrower. Their fees are usually the loan origination fee (a.k.a. points) plus some other fees, depending on the broker. They have established relationships with financial institutions that specialize in home loans and, consequently, have access to financial sources the consumer does not. Mortgage brokers must be licensed by the state and must follow the guidelines established for them by state and federal regulations.

Commercial Banks

Although a commercial bank makes loans on many types of property, home loans are most attractive because the market is large, and the home provides collateral. Moreover, for the last 20 years, commercial banks have had access to the secondary market and are becoming more active in residential housing loans. However, while commercial banks offer good interest rates, they usually have very limited programs; if you are a borrower with limited income or have credit problems, a commercial bank may not be the correct choice for you.

Mortgage Bankers (Wholesale Lenders)

Mortgage banking has been defined as the science of financing real estate transactions. Mortgage bankers originate first mortgage loans in their own name, fund them into a line of credit maintained at a commercial bank, and sell the loans to a permanent mortgage loan investor; the mortgage banker's objective is to retain the servicing of the loan. Mortgage bankers offer loans requiring 5 percent to 20 percent down payments for the home buyer, a good option for those who need a second loan for a down payment. They also offer lower interest rates and flexible programs to fit each individual's situation.

Government Financing (FHA)

The Federal Housing Administration (FHA) is part of the Department of Housing and Urban Development (HUD). Established by the National Housing Act of 1934, the purpose of the FHA is to foster home ownership in the United States as federal government policy but FHA does not make any loans. It insures the lender against defaults, meaning that it pays off the lender if the borrower does not pay the loan.

A borrower qualified for an FHA guaranteed loan can choose from different types of loans, including fixed, adjustable, and graduated payment mortgages, with terms of 15 and 30 years the most common. Still, the FHA has nothing to do with setting interest rates on a loan; it is left to the borrower and the lender to negotiate the type, term, and rate for the loan. The HUD loan limit shown in the following loan-types comparison chart is set by Congress but may differ from state to state.

The current basic standard mortgage limits for FHA insured loans are:			
One-family	Two-family	Three-family	Four-family
$172,632	$220,992	$267,120	$331,968

High-cost area limits are subject to a maximum amount based on a percent of the Freddie Mac loan limits. **The maximum amounts are currently:**			
One-family	Two-family	Three-famil	Four-family
$312,895	$400,548	$484,155	$601,692

Section 214 of the National Housing Act provides that mortgage limits for Alaska, Guam, Hawaii, and the Virgin Islands may be adjusted up to 150 percent of the new ceilings. This results in new ceilings for these areas of:			
One-family	Two-family	Three-family	Four-family
$469,342	$600,822	$726,232	$902,538

These mortgage loan limits are published by HUD field offices located in every state and county. The above shown loan limits are the most current as of December 31, 2005. Based on these limits, the maximum insurable mortgage loan is the smaller of:

- The established loan limit for the area, or

- The applicable loan-to-value (LTV) ratio applied to the smaller amount of the sale price or appraised value.

For example, if you live in Colorado Springs, Colorado, and you have been pre-qualified to buy a house for $210,000 but the house is only appraised at $208,000, and the HUD limit for that specific area is $206,798, the loan amount that FHA will guarantee is:

Maximum loan limit for that area $206,798

Sale Price $210,000

Appraised Value $208,000

Loan to Value Ratio 97 percent (Because you have to put down at least 3 percent of the sale price as shown in the loan comparison chart)

$208,000 x 3 percent = $6,240.00 down payment

$208,000 x 97 percent = $ 201,760.00 Loan to Value

The FHA guaranteed loan will be $201,760 because the appraised value is considered the final sale price even if the seller refuses to drop the price; you would have to pay the difference of $2,000.

HUD defines "Required Investment" as those funds in total to purchase, which include down payment and nonrecurring closing costs. Therefore, the above example is only explained generally with regard to the 3 percent down payment, because FHA loan guidelines include the nonrecurring closing costs plus the minimum down payment to determine the minimum investment required. Lenders use a standard factor to determine the required investment depending on the location and value or sales price of the house, because it could be in an area that has higher or lower closing costs.

The HUD guidelines acknowledge these variances under "high-cost area limits" and show a loan limit very different from the standard. States which use title and escrow companies as the settlement agents are usually low closing costs states, and those states which use attorneys for settlement agents are considered high closing costs states. The following chart lists both low and high closing costs states:

Low Closing Costs States	High Closing Costs States	
Arizona	Alabama	Montana
California	Alaska	North Carolina
Colorado	Arkansas	North Dakota
Guam	Connecticut	Nebraska
Idaho	District of Columbia	New Hampshire
Illinois	Delaware	New Jersey
Indiana	Florida	New York
New Mexico	Georgia	Ohio
Nevada	Hawaii	Oklahoma
Oregon	Iowa	Pennsylvania
Utah	Kansas	Puerto Rico
Virgin Islands	Kentucky	Rhode Island
Washington	Louisiana	South Carolina
Wisconsin	Massachusetts	South Dakota
Wyoming	Maryland	Tennessee
	Maine	Texas
	Michigan	Virginia
	Missouri	Vermont
	Minnesota	West Virginia
	Mississippi	

The required investment must be from your own funds, a genuine gift, or a loan from a family member or from a governmental agency; but it cannot come from the lender, from other sources: seller or builder. However, the closing costs may come from a builder, developer, or seller concession.

Who Can Get an FHA Guaranteed Loan?

Anyone who qualifies and has shown evidence of two years steady employment history is eligible for an FHA guaranteed loan. American citizenship is not a requirement; permanent resident aliens with proper and legitimate documentation (work permit and permanent resident alien card, both valid) are also eligible. The main condition of an FHA guaranteed loan is that the house must be used as the borrower's primary residence. Of course, you must meet standard FHA credit qualifications.

Considerations For FHA Guaranteed Loans

- **Premium Pricing.** This simply means that, through an FHA guaranteed loan, the approved lender may pay the allowable closing costs (recurring and not recurring), but the lender cannot pay for your down payment or for payment of debts, collection accounts, or liens and judgments.

- **Upfront Mortgage Insurance Premium**. This insurance is required because you are investing in your property up to 3 percent of its value or sales price. The premium will be added to the closing costs that are paid in advance and is determined by multiplying the base loan amount by the standard factor, which is 1.5 percent. Using the last example placed in Colorado, the upfront MIP is: loan amount $201,760 x factor 1.5 percent = 3,026.40. The lender could also include this premium in the mortgage.

- **Annual Mortgage Insurance Premium**. This is a premium contracted on an annual basis but paid monthly, and it is added to the mortgage loan monthly payment including taxes and hazard insurance. The annual factor is .05 percent (for less than a 15-year term), the same example the monthly installment for this insurance would be $84.07 ($201,760 x .05 percent = 1,008.80 divided by 12).

- **Escrow Account**. By FHA guidelines, an escrow account must be established for real estate taxes, hazard insurance, and, if applicable, monthly mortgage insurance and flood insurance.

- **Approved Lenders**. FHA guaranteed loans may only be obtained through HUD authorized lenders, who can be contacted directly by consumers or through mortgage brokers.

VA FINANCING

This section will explain every aspect of getting a VA loan, including eligibility requirements, advantages of a VA-guaranteed loan, examples of up front costs, applicable debt-to-income ratios, the veteran certificate, the funding fee, the appraisal, and compliance inspections.

What Is a VA Guaranteed Loan?

VA loans are guaranteed by the Department of Veterans Affairs under the Serviceman's Readjustment Act. VA guaranteed loans are awarded by private lenders such as banks, credit unions, or mortgage companies to eligible veterans for the purchase of a home used as the veteran's primary residence. Lenders rely on the VA guaranty to reduce their risk. In the event of a default, the VA promises to repay a specified amount (up to four times the Veteran's Entitlement) based upon the total loan amount. Most lenders will award VA loans to qualified veterans for up to $359,650 with no down payment required.

Like the FHA, the Veterans Administration does not give loans to veterans, but does guaranty lenders partial reimbursement of losses if the veteran does not pay back the loan. In the past, money used to pay on a defaulted loan came from the U.S. Treasury; the VA funding fee now covers this cost.

The VA does guaranty reimbursement of losses to the following extent for each loan amount:

- 50 percent of loans up to $45,000.

- From $45,000 to $144,000, a minimum guaranty of $22,500 and a maximum guaranty of up to 40 percent of the loan, but not to exceed $36,000.

- More than $144,000, the maximum guaranty is 25 percent of the home loan, not to exceed $60,000.

The only permissible loan products for VA guaranteed loans are:

- The fixed rate mortgage, with terms for 15 and 30 years, where 30 years is the most common.

- Graduated payment mortgage.

- Buy-down.

- Growing equity mortgage.

The VA has nothing to do with interest rates or loan limits; the lender sets the loan limits based on what is stipulated by Ginnie Mae, and the veteran and lender negotiate the type of loan, term, and rate.

Normally, the type of property a veteran may purchase is a single family residence or detached property, but if a veteran wants to purchase an attached property such as a condo, townhouse, or Planned Unit Development (PUD), the purchase can be submitted to the VA for approval.

Advantages of VA Guaranteed Loans

VA loans do have less restrictive qualifying conditions compared to conventional loans, but those are not their only advantages:

- No down payment, unless it is required by the lender (which is not common) or the sale price of the house is more than the reasonable value.

- Negotiable interest rates.

- Veterans can finance the VA funding fee: the fee can

be rolled over into the amount to be financed. If the veteran does make a down payment of at least 5 percent, the funding fee can be reduced. An exemption to the fee might also be granted for veterans receiving VA compensation for a service-connected disability.

- Closing costs are the same or even lower than other types of loans.

- Veterans do not have to pay mortgage insurance.

- No prepayment penalty is assessed should the veteran wish to pay off the loan before its maturity.

- Seller/builder/developer can pay up to 100 percent of all the veteran's closing costs.

Who Can Get a VA Guaranteed Loan?

All veterans honorably discharged or released from active duty and meeting certain military service requirements are eligible for the VA loan program. The military service requirements are as follows:

1. **Wartime Service.** Includes military service during World War II, the Korean conflict, or the Vietnam Era or at least 90 days on active duty and an honorable discharge or release. Veterans may also be eligible if discharged for a service-connected disability.

2. **Peacetime Service.** Veteran must have served at least 181 days of continuous active duty during specifically designated periods.

3. **Service after September 7, 1980 (enlisted personnel)**

or October 16, 1981 (officers) and prior to August 2, 1990. Veterans separated from service which began after these dates must have completed 24 months of continuous active duty for the full period that they were called or ordered to active duty. Individuals may also be eligible if they were released from active duty due to an involuntary reduction in force, certain medical conditions, or in some cases for the convenience of the government.

4. **Gulf War.** Individuals who served on active duty during the Gulf War must have completed 24 months of continuous active duty or the full period for which they were called or ordered to active duty or completed at least 90 days of active duty and been discharged by a "hardship discharge" or "early out discharge" or have been determined to have a service-connected disability or, if they served less than 90 days, discharged due to a service-connected disability.

5. **Active Duty Service Personnel.** Individuals who are currently on active duty and have served on continuous active duty for at least 181 days (90 days during the Persian Gulf War) unless discharged or separated from a previous period of active duty service.

6. **Selected Reserve.** Individuals who do not fall into the above-mentioned circumstances but have completed a total of six years in the Selected Reserves or National Guard (member of an active unit, attended required weekend drills and two-week active duty training) and either were honorably discharged, were placed on the retired list, or were transferred to the Standby Reserve or

an element of the Ready Reserve other than the Selected Reserve after an honorable service or who continue to serve in the Selected Reserve. In addition, individuals who completed less than six years may be eligible for a VA loan if discharged for a service-connected disability.

Unmarried surviving spouses of eligible veterans (that meet service requirements) may also be eligible for VA Loan Guaranty benefits under the following circumstances:

- When veteran has died as a result of service-connected cause.

- Spouse of an active duty member who is listed as missing in action or a prisoner of war for at least 90 days.

Veteran Certificate of Eligibility

The VA determines your eligibility and, if you are qualified, will issue you a certificate of eligibility to be used in applying for a VA loan. Should you need to request a certificate from the VA, you must complete VA Form 26-1880, "Request for a Certificate of Eligibility for VA Home Loan Benefits" and submit it to one of the VA Eligibility Centers along with acceptable proof of service as described on the instruction page of the form. In some cases, eligible veterans will receive a Certificate of Eligibility upon discharge. Members of the Reserves and National Guard who do not possess a Certificate must also submit the form to the VA.

Veteran's Entitlement

The Certificate of Eligibility will show the amount of the entitlement available to you as an eligible Veteran. The maximum loan entitlement to any veteran is $36,000, but an additional $24,000 of entitlement is available for loans of more than $144,000, as explained previously.

What Is the Funding Fee?

A VA funding fee of 2 percent of the loan amount (2.75 percent for reservists) is also payable at the time of loan closing. This fee may be included in the loan and paid from the loan monies as long as the total loan amount does not exceed the VA loan limit. The funding fee is not required of veterans receiving VA compensation for service-connected disabilities, or who, but for the receipt of retirement pay, would be entitled to receive compensation for service-connected disabilities or surviving spouses of veterans who died in service or from a service-connected disability. If the veteran makes a down payment of at least 5 percent but less than 10 percent of the purchase price of the property, the funding fee is reduced to 1.5 percent of the loan amount (2.25 percent for reservists). If the veteran makes a down payment of at least 10 percent, the funding fee is reduced to 1.25 percent of the loan amount (2 percent for reservists). If a veteran who has previously obtained a VA home loan obtains another loan with less than a 5 percent down payment, the funding fee is 3 percent of the loan amount.

The Appraisal

Appraisal of the subject property must be conducted by VA-approved appraisers. VA uses a Reasonable Property Value to calculate the amount guaranteed and to determine if the sales price is within the loan limits. As in a FHA guaranteed loan, if the Reasonable Property Value is lower than the sales price, the veteran must make up to the total price.

Closing Costs That Are Allowed

VA guaranteed loans allow the seller/builder/developer to give concessions to the veteran to assist the buyer in paying closing costs (no more than 4 percent of the value). After the closing, the veteran may get money back, but the amount must not be more than the total for what he/she put down or placed as an earnest money deposit, and fees paid prior to the close of escrow, as long as those fees were part of the actual acquisition of the loan—a credit report or appraisal, for example—may also be reimbursed.

In compliance with VA guidelines, the allowed and most common closing costs include, but are not limited to:

- VA appraisal

- Credit report

- Survey

- Title report

- Recording fees

- 1 percent origination loan fee

- Discount points, in case the veteran does want to pay points in order to get a better interest rate.

As previously discussed, getting a mortgage loan can be very expensive. It is for that reason that the VA regulates closing costs. As you can see in the above list, only those costs that are imposed while obtaining a VA loan may be levied, but commissions or broker fees often demanded when applying for a conventional loan are not permitted.

The closing costs and origination fee may not be included in the loan except in VA refinancing loans.

Debt-to-Income Ratio

Shown in the loan-type comparison chart is a 50 percent for DTI Ratio. However, the maximum DTI Ratio determined by VA guidelines is 41 percent. Therefore, any veteran applying for a loan with a DTI of more than 41 percent may not qualify unless there are extenuating circumstances. Some lenders may qualify a veteran for a VA guaranteed loan when the DTI ratio is higher than that established if residual income is high.

What is Residual Income?

The VA is always concerned about a veteran's ability to pay the maintenance and utilities for the property he or she intends to purchase and, consequently, includes in its guidelines a calculation for residual income. Residual income is the amount of income available for family support after taxes and social security expenses have been subtracted from the gross income and after the housing monthly payment (this procedure is not performed in conventional loans) and payment of other long-term debt (to be paid in more than 10 monthly installments).

What Is Not Guaranteed by the VA?

There are some things that a veteran must consider very carefully when applying for a VA guaranteed loan. As with any loan, it is ultimately up to the buyer to understand the limitations of many of the provisions of the loan and the loan process. While the VA does protect veterans and provide better opportunities for veterans who wish to purchase a home, there are some things the VA does not do:

- Since the VA only guarantees the loan, it cannot guarantee that a property is defect-free. A VA appraisal is not intended to be an inspection of the property, so seeking expert advice from a qualified residential inspector is highly recommended.

- If a veteran is building his or her home, the VA cannot tell the builder to correct construction defects, but it does have the authority to suspend a builder from further participation in the VA home loan program.

- The VA cannot provide a veteran with legal services.

USING AN IRA OR OTHER RETIREMENT PLAN

This section deals with the use of funds from a retirement plan to cover some of the costs that accrue when purchasing or building a home.

What Is a Retirement Plan?

This section provides only a general overview of the retirement plans that may be used to support your loan application process. For mortgage purposes, they are handled equally, but for tax purposes they are handled in different ways depending of the type of retirement plan.

- **Defined Contribution Plan.** This plan is an employer's stock bonus, pension, or profit-sharing plan that is only for the benefit of employees or their beneficiaries. The employer may contribute as well as the employee. This type is often referred to as a 401(k) (for private companies), a 403(b) (for public school employees), and, for governmental employees, the Thrift Savings Plan or other designation.

- **Simplified Employee Pension plans (SEP).** These plans do not commit the employer to annual contributions. The contribution amount is usually limited to 25 percent of employee compensation for small business employees and 20 percent for self-employed individuals.

- **Savings Incentive Match Plans for Employees (SIMPLE).** SIMPLE plans are intended for employers with 100 or fewer eligible employees. Employee eligibility is based on the reasonable expectation of earning at least $5,000 in compensation during the current year and on earnings of at least $5,000 in any two preceding years, consecutive or not.

- **Individual Retirement Account (IRA).** This is a trust or custodial account set up in the United States with a financial or investment institution for the exclusive benefit of the account holder and beneficiaries. The account is created by a written document and must meet specific terms of disbursement.

- **Keogh.** These are also defined contribution plans, but are called Keogh plans if they are maintained by a self-employed individual.

In Chapter 6, you learned that having a retirement plan could be very beneficial because it can be used to pay closing costs or a down payment, or it might be presented as proof of financial reserves. As a financial reserve, disbursement is not necessary, but if you need to withdraw funds from your retirement funds for use in purchasing a home or to make payments (there are almost always limitations on withdrawals as well as exemptions, like hardship due to health problems, that override limitations), there are things you will have to provide or do, especially if you are first-time home buyer.

For the Lender

- Proof of the distribution from a retirement plan. You must show written proof (a bank statement) of your retirement plan and the deposit or automated transfer made from the retirement account to your checking or savings account. Remember that some lenders require that the money is both sourced and seasoned.

- Proof of retirement plan to show reserves. You must provide written proof (a bank statement) for the retirement plan.

For the Internal Revenue Service (IRS)

Usually, when disbursements are made from your retirement plan, federal income tax is withheld by the managing institution because that money is then treated as taxable income having been originally set aside as tax-deferred income, but when you use those monies to purchase your first home, the IRS allows certain exceptions.

- **Retirement plans.** If you borrow money from your retirement plan, it is treated as a non-periodic distribution (you would have to pay federal income tax, normally 20 percent of the distribution amount) unless it used to buy your main home. This exception applies to 401(k), 403(b), and governmental plan loans. The non-periodic distribution can be up to $50,000

- **Individual Retirement Accounts.** Normally, when an individual makes a distribution from his or her IRA before age 59½, it is treated as received income, and that distribution will be subject to federal withholding tax (regular plus a penalty of 10 percent). However, when individuals use that distribution to buy, build, or rebuild their first home, the money received is exempt from withholding tax, though the first-time homebuyer must meet all the following requirements:

  - The money must be used to pay qualified acquisition costs (costs of buying, building, or rebuilding a home and any usual or reasonable settlement, financing, or other closing costs) before the close of the 120th day after the day you received it.

  - It must be used to pay for qualified acquisition costs for the main home (primary residence) of a first-time homebuyer who is any of the following:

    - The IRA account holder.

    - The spouse of the IRA holder.

    - Child or spouse's child of the IRA holder.

    - Grandchild of IRA holder or holder's spouse.

    - Parent or other ancestor of IRA holder or of spouse.

An individual is considered a first-time homebuyer under

IRS rules if he or she has no present interest in a main home during the two-year period ending on the date of acquisition[23] of the home for which the distribution is being used to buy, build or rebuild; and if married, the spouse must also meet this no-ownership requirement.

- When added to all prior qualified first-time homebuyer distributions, if any, the total distributions cannot be more than $10,000, but if you are married both you and your spouse can receive distributions up to the said amount.

[22]Date of acquisition is the date that (a) you entered into a binding contract to buy the main home for which the distribution is being used or (b) the building or rebuilding of the main home for which the distribution is being used begins.

8

THE CLOSING–
A PRACTICAL VIEW

In the preceding chapters, you learned the process of applying for your loan from initial application to lender approval, but before closing, there may be further conditions that must be met to satisfy the loan officer. In fact, that is usually the case, particularly if you have applied for a nonconforming loan that requires more creative financing and, consequently, more documentation and verification of the details of your application. It is not uncommon for closing dates to be delayed so the loan officer can dot every "i" and cross every "t".

There are things you should do as well:

- Make a final walk-through inspection. This is your last chance to check for additional problems or needed repairs. If repairs were a condition of sale, it is also your last chance to ensure that they the work has been done to your satisfaction. Make a checklist based on previous agreements and take it with you to see if the house is in the condition you expected and that all items, such as appliances, water heaters, and so forth, are in the house and in acceptable condition. If the seller has not met the conditions of sale, some of the monies that will go to the seller may be held in an escrow account until agreed-upon actions are completed.

- Schedule closing at the end of the month. Prepaid interest will be included in your closing costs because mortgage interest is paid after the month has passed (arrears). Consequently, following the closing you will have a whole month's delay before the first full mortgage payment is due. For example, if you pay $20 in loan interest daily and your closing occurs on January 15, the amount of prepaid interest you pay is $300 ($20 daily-interest x 15 days = $300). Your first payment is due March 1. On the other hand, if the close of escrow is on January 30, you only have to pay interest for two days (the 30th and 31st), and the due date for the first mortgage payment is still March 1. By scheduling your closing late in the month, you reduce your closing costs.

CLOSING COSTS AND TITLE FEES (NONRECURRING FEES)

The following "settlement fees" are the most common nonrecurring fees, but they may vary from state to state and some from county to county; some can be negotiated. For reference, see the Good Faith Estimate sample included in Appendix C.

Items Payable in Connection With the Loan

These are fees lenders charge to process, approve, and make the loan.

- **Loan origination fee.** This fee covers the lenders or broker's administrative costs in processing the loan and is often expressed as a percent of the loan, though the fees vary among lenders. Usually it is 1 percent of the loan amount, but could be up to 2 percent if the loan amount is below $50,000.

- **Loan discount.** It is often referred to as "discount points" because it is charged when the borrower chooses to lower the interest rate for which he or she is qualified in order to get lower monthly payments. One "point" is equal to 1 percent of the loan amount. For example, if a borrower were qualified for an interest rate of 6.5 percent on a $150,000 loan but determined that the resulting monthly payment would be too high, either the lender or borrower might elect to lower the rate to 5.5 percent but include discount points of 1 percent, or $1,500 in the total of the closing costs. Points are negotiable along with the amount of the origination fee.

- **Appraisal fee.** This fee is paid by you at the time the property is appraised, but has to be disclosed in the Good Faith Estimate (GFE). The fee ranges from $350 to $450.

- **Credit report fee**. Paid at the time you apply for the mortgage loan and disclosed in the GFE. The payment goes to the credit reporting agency used by the lender or broker. The fee varies from $16 to $24.

- **Lender's inspection fees.** These are only charged when the loan is for construction; each inspection fee could be from $70 to $80.

- **Mortgage insurance application fees.** This fee covers the processing of the application for Private Mortgage Insurance (PMI), if it applies.

- **Assumption fee.** This fee is charged to process documents on loans freely assumable.

- **Mortgage broker fees.** Applicable if a mortgage broker is retained and is paid to the broker or brokerage company. This fee varies throughout the country and could be from $600 to $1,000.

- **Tax-related service fee.** Applicable if the lender requires the borrower's tax returns. The fee is usually from $80 to $110.

- **Underwriting fee.** This fee is charged by the lender for evaluating the loan application and for services leading to the approval of the loan. It ranges from $450 to $995.

- **Processing fee.** Goes to the mortgage broker or lender and is usually from $200 to $550.

- **Wire transfer fee.** This fee covers costs of transferring money to the escrow agent. It is paid to the lender and varies from $15 to $20.

- **Postage/Special Delivery Fee**. This fee covers the costs of express delivery of documents — $30 to $50.

Title Charges

Title charges cover a variety of services performed by title companies and others including transfer of title, title search, document preparation, and it covers fees for title insurance and legal fees if you use an attorney as the escrow agent.

- **Closing or escrow fee.** Paid to the escrow agent (escrow company or attorney). Every agent has pre-determined fees based on the loan amount. The seller has to pay half of this fee in accordance with the purchase contract.

- **Abstract or title search**. Cost of search and examination of records of previous ownership and transfers of title to determine if the seller is the actual owner of the property. In western states, because the escrow and title company are the same, the escrow fee includes this service; therefore, this fee may not be part of the closing costs.

- **Title examination fee**. This fee is a pass-on fee for the services of an outside title examiner.

- **Document preparation fee.** There may be a separate document fee covering the costs of preparation for documents including a mortgage, warranty deed, deed of trust, promissory note, deed, and transfer of title.

- **Notary Fee.** Paid to a public notary for notarizing certain documents.

- **Attorney's fees**. Charged by the lender in connection with legal services provided to examine the title binder, sales contract, or the construction contract for a construction loan.

- **Title Insurance**. This is a one-time premium usually paid for the lender's title insurance coverage. Upon signing the purchase agreement, the seller pays the owner's title insurance.

- Other title or escrow charges.

Government Recording and Transfer Charges

Either you or the seller may pay these fees depending upon the purchase contract. These are fees the county recorder charges for recording the transfer and mortgage documents.

- Recording fees are charged by the county recorder for legally recording the new deed and mortgage; fees vary in every county.

- City/County Tax Stamps. The respective city or county tax authority determines this fee.

- State Tax Stamps. The state tax authority determines this fee.

Additional Settlement Charges

These are charges that may be determined by the lender in each specific case and may also be paid by either the buyer or seller depending on the terms of the purchase contract.

- **Flood hazard determination certification fee.** Some lenders require flood hazard determination to make sure the subject property is not located in a flood zone--$15 to $20.

- **Pest inspection.** If this inspection is not waived at the execution of the purchase contract, either you or the seller will pay this fee.

- **Survey fee**. This is only in case of construction, but if it applies, you will have to pay this fee which goes to the surveyor.

THE UP-FRONT COSTS (RECURRING CHARGES)

Prepaid recurring charges are paid to the lender and others through escrow. These charges include, if applicable, interest for the number of days between the closing of escrow and the first monthly payment (accrued interest), the mortgage insurance premium, private mortgage insurance, the hazard insurance premium, the VA funding fee, and reserves placed on account with the lender.

Items required by the lender to be paid in advance:

- **Interest.** Lenders usually require that borrowers pay at settlement the interest that accrues on the mortgage from the date of settlement to the beginning of the period covered by the first monthly payment. Daily interest is determined by multiplying the interest rate times the loan amount and dividing by 360 or 365.

- **The FHA one-time mortgage insurance premium (MIP)** or the VA funding fee. These fees go to the mortgage insurance company and the VA Loan Service Agency, respectively.

- **The hazard insurance premium**. This item is a one-year prepayment and must be paid at settlement to ensure proper coverage for the subject property.

- **Flood insurance premium.** This is also a one-year prepayment and is required if the subject property is determined to be in a flood zone.

- **Private mortgage insurance.** If applicable, PIM is paid to the mortgage insurance company. The amount is calculated by multiplying the factor shown in the loan type comparison chart by the loan amount.

- Other items required by the lender to meet the conditions of loan approval. They might include tax liens, judgments, and other obligations stemming from legal actions that could result in an encumbrance on the property.

Reserves Deposited with the Lender

Also known as escrow, reserves are held in an "escrow" account by the lender to assure future payment for recurring items such as real estate taxes, hazard insurance, mortgage insurance premiums, and so forth. These reserves may have to be deposited with the lender depending on the type of loan that has awarded. If the loan is impounded, they will be included with the principal and interest monthly payment and deposited in an escrow account; normally, impounded funds are for the hazard insurance premiums, mortgage insurance premium, property taxes, flood insurance, and other local taxes that may apply, depending on the state.

- **Hazard insurance premiums.** The lender determines the amount of money to be placed in reserve for the next insurance premium. It is based on the homeowner's insurance premium and the number of payments that must be held in reserve — usually two or three — as determined by the lender.

- **Mortgage insurance premium or private mortgage insurance reserves**. These are handled identically to reserves for hazard insurance.

- **Flood insurance reserves**. These are also handled identically to the reserves for hazard insurance but are only applicable if the property is located in a flood zone.

- **Taxes and assessment reserves**. These are also required to ensure the future payment of real estate taxes and value assessments on the property; lenders usually require three months in advance.

- Any other local tax related to property ownership, e.g, a school tax.

CALCULATING THE MONTHLY PAYMENTS

Earlier in the book we explained how to estimate your monthly payments. Now that you are familiar with the entire buying process, the explanation of calculating your payments found in the following example might be helpful.

Conventional conforming loan (less than loan limits and with good credit score).

Sales price: $226,040

First loan amount: $169,530 (75 percent loan to value)

Second loan amount: $56,510 (25 percent loan to value)

Interest rate first loan: 6.675 percent

Interest rate second loan: 8.5 percent

Estimated annual taxes: $2,200

Estimated hazard insurance annual premium: $720

Fixed rate for 30 years

Taxes and insurance are impounded and will be added to the monthly payment

Monthly payment will include principal and interest

Property is located in Garland (Dallas County), Texas

Mortgage Loan Monthly Payment Calculation (Estimated)

Concept	Amount
Principal and interest	$1,091.13
Other financing (2nd loan)	$434.51
Hazard insurance ($720 divided by 12)	$60.00
Real estate taxes ($2,200 divided by 12)	$183.33
Total estimated monthly payment	$1,768.97

TYPES OF TITLES TO PROPERTY

At closing, the rights to property are transferred with the title to the property. It's important, therefore, that you understand the definitions of the different types of title to property.

Real Property Estates

In a mortgage, the real property owner gives the lender an interest in the property to protect the lender in the event the borrower fails to repay the loan as agreed (default). After pledging the property as a security for the loan (collateral), the borrower retains certain rights to the property. Keep in mind that no one owns land, they simply own certain rights to the land, including possession, and these rights might be shared. The term "estate" is used to describe the borrower's rights and interest in real property.

There are two types of estates:

1. Fee simple estate

2. Leasehold estate

Fee Simple Estate

In this kind of estate, the owner is entitled to the property and all rights committed with it. This allows the owner to sell, mortgage, lease, make improvements to, or sell his or her rights such as water, mineral, air, or timber. If one of the owners dies, the title to the property passes to his or her descendants. The most common forms of ownership are:

- **Sole ownership**. Only one individual has rights and interest to the property; this applies to single individuals when applied for a loan individually.

- **Joint tenancy.** This is the most common form of ownership for couples, married or not. Under this form, each person owns an undivided[24] interest in the property; at the death of one joint tenant, the interest is immediately transferred to the surviving owner who then becomes the sole owner of the property.

- **Tenancy by the entirety.** This form of ownership operates similarly to joint tenancy but requires that the tenants be spouses and that the property is their homestead. This form of ownership is not recognized in some states.

Tenancy by the entirety is also defined in some states as community property, among them Alaska, Wisconsin, Louisiana, Texas, New Mexico, Arizona, Idaho, Nevada, Washington, California, and Puerto Rico. In those jurisdictions, a special definition of the husband-wife relationship is implemented based on Spanish or Napoleonic law, because Spain or France first colonized those states. These states consider any property acquired during a marriage, except by gift or inheritance, to be community property, meaning each spouse owns half of the property. In some states, community property has rights of survivorship similar to joint tenancy. In a community property state, the law presumes that all property acquired during the marriage by the efforts of either spouse is community property unless the deed indicates otherwise.

[23]This means that if there are three joint tenants, each owns an undivided interest in the whole and not just one-third part of the property.

Exemptions are usually declared in a quitclaim deed in which one of the spouses renounces certain rights to the property. If you and your spouse purchase a house but only one of you applied for the loan, the lender may require you to file a quitclaim deed as a condition for loan approval.

- **Tenancy in common**. This form gives each owner separate legal title to an undivided interest in the property and allows the owners the right to sell, mortgage or give away their own interest in the property subject to the continuing interests of the other owner(s). When one owner dies, the interest in the property does not pass to the other owner(s), but it does pass by inheritance to the beneficiaries established in will or succession.

Sole ownership, joint tenancy, and tenancy in common are used in all states, but certain specific details of ownership might vary by state. Tenancy by the entirety is available in about 40 percent of the states, most of them in the eastern portion of the country.

Leasehold Estate

A leasehold estate is created when the owner of the property grants the tenant the right to a piece of land for a period of time. In this case, lenders provide leasehold financing when an individual requests a loan to buy, build a home, or build on land that is rented.[25]

---

[24]Refer to Land Contract explained in Chapter 3.

THE CLOSING

Prior to the Closing:

- Confirm the amount required for closing costs and get a certified or cashier's check for that amount issued by a local financial institution. Do not rely on personal checks since the law requires the escrow agent to have secure funds before making disbursements from escrow. Since these funds are placed in escrow to be disbursed to other parties in the transaction, the escrow agent responsible for those payments is not likely to accept anything other than a certified check.

- Confirm that the insurance binder for hazard insurance and other applicable insurance coverages is already in the hands of the escrow agent. You must have the appropriate insurance coverage in place before the lender can release funds to the escrow agent.

- Get a valid form of identification that must be shown for your signature to be notarized during the closing.

- Decide whether you want a lawyer or other professional present during the closing, keeping in mind the escrow agent cannot give legal advice on any matter pertaining to the transaction.

- See additional actions you should take in Chapter 9 in anticipation of moving into your new home.

At the Closing:

Be sure to review and read all documents.

- Reviewed HUD-1 (contains all itemized closing costs and funds needed from buyer to close the transaction).

- Mortgage deed/warranty deed/deed of trust/ promissory note.

- Note riders.

- Deed or Title.

- Final GFE and TIL.

- All other documents that are part of the closing process.

After the Closing

An escrow closing is a legal transfer of title to property from a seller to a buyer and is the culmination of the home purchase transaction. After you have signed all the necessary instructions and documents, the escrow agent will return them to the lender for a final review. Once assured everything is in order, the lender informs the escrow agent that the loan will be funded so required procedures can be completed to record the documents and close the escrow.

When the public instruments are recorded, usually within one business day of the escrow agent's receipt of loan funds, the transaction is complete and the agent declares the "close of escrow" (COE).

The keys to your new house will then be handed over to you by the listing agent.

After all documents are recorded, the escrow agent will contact you to deliver certified copies of some of the documents you signed at closing, and your deed will be mailed directly to you by the county recorder's office.

Congratulations! At this point, you are the owners of your own home.

9

THE NEXT STEPS FOLLOWING THE PURCHASE OF YOUR HOME

MOVING IN

Preparations for Moving In

- At least two weeks in advance order utilities hook-up for a date following the closing and arrange for a rental truck or for movers.

- Give your current landlord notice in accordance with the terms of your lease.

- Talk to your real estate agent to make arrangements for picking up the house keys.

Deductible Expenses for Tax Purposes

According to IRS regulations, if the move to a new house is job-related, and your new home is more than a certain number of miles from your old home, you may be able to deduct many of your moving costs. Consult with your accountant; should you meet the IRS definition of a qualifying move, you may be able to deduct the following:

- The cost of traveling to the area where a new job is located to look for a home. A home purchase is not necessarily required for that expense to be deductible.

- The cost of having your furniture and other household items shipped, including the cost of packing, insurance, and storage (up to 30 days).

- The cost of transporting your family to the new location; this includes food and lodging expenses during the trip.

- Costs necessitated by a delay in finding a new home or as a result of the home not being ready for occupancy (the cost of lodging and 80 percent of food expenses for up to 30 days).

REBUILD YOUR SAVINGS

When you decided to purchase a home, you also found that putting your finances in order was absolutely necessary to be awarded a home loan. Don't stop now, particularly if you were forced to pay a large sum for the down payment and closing costs, causing you to deplete your savings or other liquid assets. Most important is developing a good budget that takes into account the expenses associated with home ownership and sticking to it.

Some items on that budget are already taken care of for you. Payments for home insurance and property taxes are held in escrow by your lender; you need only pay your mortgage payment, which includes funds set aside for insurance and taxes, on time. Nevertheless, it is your responsibility to ensure that those funds are properly handled and the tax and insurance payments are made. After you've paid the mortgage in full, you will have to set aside those funds yourself and make payment.

A real danger to homeowners is consumer credit and credit cards. It is all too easy to think they should be used to purchase household items or to pay bills when those items are not really needed and household income is not going to be enough to handle credit card payments including what is usually exorbitant interest. Use credit cards for emergencies only, where your house is concerned, and charge only those balances you will be able to pay off each month.

When major maintenance or repairs become inevitable, you may be able to recapitalize your equity in a home equity loan or home equity line of credit that carry lower interest rates and allow the deduction of loan interest from your taxes.

Home warranty protection is a very prudent investment that could save you thousands in unexpected expenses. If the seller has not included such protection in the deal, you may want to purchase it yourself. This policy protects you as a buyer by paying for certain repairs within a period of time following the assumption of ownership.

Some advantages of the home warranty protection are:

- Protects cash flow.

- Puts a complete network of qualified service technicians at your service.

- Low deductible.

Ask your real estate agent to explain options on plans or refer you to a company offering such protection.

Never make a late payment on your mortgage. The mortgage should always be your highest priority when paying bills—you can do without everything else, but not a home. Moreover, being late on mortgage payments will damage your credit rating and cause serious problems for you if you want to refinance your home later or apply for a loan to purchase another house. Lenders charge a percent of the monthly payment as penalty for late fees.

MORTGAGE INSURANCE

If you want to protect your family in the event of your death, mortgage insurance might be a smart option, but shop around; not all offers for mortgage insurance are sound investments. Consult your real estate professionals for referrals.

What is Mortgage Insurance Protection?

Mortgage life insurance pays the unpaid balance of the loan amount in the event of the borrower's death, though, depending on the provisions of the policy, it may also cover the borrower for loss of employment or hardship. Depending on the type of policy, the insurance might be treated as an investment which is returned at the end of the contract (usually 10 years).

How Much Should You Pay For It?

The difference between regular life insurance and mortgage life insurance is that while life insurance provides money for named beneficiaries, mortgage insurance pays your lender directly. Premiums for mortgage insurance, depending on your age and health habits, could range from $10 to $80 a month.

Ignore Offers for Quicker Mortgage Payoffs and Refinance

As a homeowner, you will discover that all kinds of people will suddenly have an interest in you. Your mailbox will soon be full of offers for refinancing and strategies for faster payoff. To be blunt, what should come to your mind immediately is the old adage of "buyer beware."

Early payoffs can more easily be arranged by contacting your existing lender when the time is right. An early payoff plan is essentially a graduated payment mortgage. If that sounds interesting to you, contact your lender or broker (after a specified period of time if your mortgage loan has a prepay penalty) and ask how you can get this option, but do your homework first, and be very aware that early payoffs, or refinancing, for that matter, can increase your monthly payments considerably.

Consider Refinancing Your Mortgage

Refinancing may be a good option to lower monthly payments or get cash out of the home equity.

Refinancing to Lower Payments

If interest rates have fallen since you took out a fixed-rate home loan, you might want to refinance your loan. Since closing costs on the refinanced loan and prepayment penalties on your existing loan will offset some of your savings, the general guideline is for the new interest rate to be at least two points lower than your existing rate. It is prudent to lower the time of the loan to less than the remaining time of the loan.

If you have an adjustable-rate mortgage and the fixed-rate period is over, refinancing is recommended because your interest rate is now free to rise. A fixed rate mortgage is a good option at this point, particularly if the interest rates are expected to rise more than two points above your existing rate. With an ARM, that is very likely.

Refinance Cash-Out

This option is for homeowners who need money to face high debt, need to make major improvements to the house, or need funds for other expenditures. You will need to determine your equity in the house first by comparing the values of comparable homes in your area to estimate market value and deducting the amount you still owe on the loan. The amount you can borrow against your equity is a percentage of the result. Closing costs to refinance may be deducted as well.

For a first-time homebuyer, an agent is crucial in the purchasing process. Since the first-time buyer has never been through the process, he needs someone who knows the process, someone to point out what to look for, and someone to help him figure out what is normal and what isn't. The majority of homebuyers – whether they're going to purchase their first home or their fifth home – do not know their rights, so an agent will help them understand the process and their rights.

I always encourage home buyers to get pre-qualified before searching for a home, especially a first-time homebuyer. Many home buyers think they can afford a certain amount when, in reality, they can not. For example, a home buyer may think he can afford a $200,000 dollar home. However, buyers tend to forget about additional costs, including closing costs, taxes, mortgage insurance, and many other items that figure into the monthly payment. I always say, unless you are an expert in real estate, find and ask an expert.

I have a referral relationship with a lender I trust. I want to send my clients to someone I can trust to charge a fair amount and who will get the job done on time and right.

The average price for a single family home in my area is about $260,000, although a year ago it was around $200,000. PUD homes are most common for first-time buyers because they are generally more affordable.

I recently sold a home to a family who had never bought a home before. They were wary whether they were making the right choice because they didn't know whether they could afford the home, even though they already spoke with a lender. When I took them to look at different homes, they seemed so eager to buy that any house was fine.

After we viewed a house, they decided they wanted to make an offer. However, I pushed them to see the next house, so they knew what was out there in their price range. I wanted them to choose the right house. They finally made the decision to make an offer on a particular house, and when we did the inspection problems came up. They were so overwhelmed by this time that they didn't know what to do. I told them to go home, and I would prepare the correct paperwork to have the seller fix everything. Finally, the house closed. They are now so excited and happy about their new home, they've told all of their family and friends how easy I made the whole transaction. And many of their friends and family now want to become homeowners.

Most of the time, a first-time buyer doesn't know there is the possibility of a buyer-agent relationship written agreement. However, I show the agreement to them, explain what it is, and I ask them to sign it. Essentially, by signing it they're telling me I am the only agent with whom they can and will work. I also tell them that by signing the contract, they are serious and respect me and my time. If they sign the contract, I will work 110 percent for them.

I explain the home-buying process to my buyers. I normally give the abridged version and ask my buyers if they understand or have any questions. I do this because I believe that if I go too much into detail, people get overwhelmed and become scared. I want my buyers to relax and know they are in good hands.

It depends on the circumstances whether I ask the sellers to pay for the buyers' closing costs. You can ask on any transaction, but sometimes it hurts the buyer to ask for some closing costs.

I have been in the real estate business for almost a year now. I know that isn't long at all, but you have to understand the environment I work in. I am in a top producing office; everyone in my office is experienced and knowledgeable. We are not just a bunch of agents competing against each other like most offices. At the same time, we are not a team.

I view my office as a family, because we all get along, look after each others' children, and look after each other. If one person in our office needs help, the whole office is there to give support and advice. For me as a newer agent, I couldn't be in a better place. When I have a question or need help on a transaction, I can talk to anyone in my office. When you hire me as your agent, you are not just getting me; you are getting a family, a family full of knowledge and experience.

Adam Springer

The mortgage should always be your highest priority when paying bills.

REAL ESTATE GLOSSARY

Abandonment: The renouncement of all rights and title to a property with no intention of reclaiming ownership.

Abstract of title: A condensed history or digest of the title to a parcel of land consisting of a summary of every recorded instrument, together with a statement of all liens, charges, or encumbrances affecting title to that land.

Acceleration clause: A clause in a mortgage or agreement of sale stating that upon default of a payment due, immediate and full payment of the balance of the obligation becomes due and payable.

Accelerated cost recovery system: A tax procedure that provides greater depreciation in the early years of ownership of real estate or personal property.

Acceptance: The seller's written approval of a buyer's offer.

Accessibility: The degree to which a building or site allows access to people with disabilities.

Acknowledgement: A written declaration affirming that an individual acted voluntarily.

Acre: A measurement of land equal to 43,560 feet.

Acre foot: The volume of material needed to cover an acre of land one foot deep.

Actual age: The number of years a structure has been standing.

Addendum: An addition or change to a contract.

Agency: The legal relationship resulting from an agreement where the agent is authorized to perform certain acts on behalf of the principal in dealing with a third party.

Agreement of sale: A written agreement in which the buyer agrees to buy certain property and the seller agrees to sell upon terms and conditions. Title remains with the seller until terms and conditions are fulfilled; buyer has equitable title.

Appraisal: An estimate of value of real estate; the report stating and supporting the estimated value of realty.

Appreciation: An increased value of property due to economic or related causes which may prove to be either temporary or permanent.

Assessment: A charge against real estate made by a unit of government or a condo association to cover the proportionate cost of improvement.

Assignment: The method or manner by which a right or contract is transferred from one person to another.

Adjusted cost basis: The cost of any improvements the seller makes to the property.

Ad valorem tax: A tax levied according to value, generally used to refer to real estate tax, also called the general tax.

Administrator: A person given authority to manage and distribute the estate of someone who died.

Administrator's deed: A legal document that an administrator of an estate uses to transfer property.

Adverse use: The access and use of property without the owner's consent.

Aeolian soil: Soil that is composed of materials deposited by the wind.

Affiant: An individual who makes a sworn statement.

A-Frame design: An interior style that features a steeply peaked roofline and a ceiling that is open to the top rafters.

Agent: A person licensed by the state to conduct real estate transactions.

Alcove: A recessed section of a room, such as a breakfast nook.

Alkali: Mineral salt found in soil.

Alkaline soil: Soil that contains a higher concentration of mineral salt than natural acid.

Allowances: Budgets offered by builders of new homes for the purchase of carpeting and fixtures.

Aluminum Siding: A metal covering that provides an alternative to paint for owners of wood homes.

Aluminum-clad windows: Wooden windows with aluminum covering the exterior.

American Land Title Association (ALTA) policy: A title insurance policy that protects the interest in a collateral property of a mortgage lender who originates a new real estate loan.

Amenities: Parks, swimming pools, health-club facilities, party rooms, bike paths, community centers, and other attractions offered by builders of planned developments.

Amperage: The strength of an electrical current.

Anchor bolt: A large steel bolt anchored in concrete and attached to a building framing to prevent the structure from moving.

Annual: Any kind of plant that must be planted every year.

Appraisal report: A detailed written report on the value of a property based on recent sales of comparable sites in the area.

Appraised value: An opinion of the current market value of a property.

Arbitration: A method of resolving a dispute in which a third party renders a decision.

Architectural fees: The fee architects charge for services. They generally charge by the hour, by the square foot, or by a percentage of the project budget.

Asbestos: A fire-resistant mineral used for insulation and home products that has been found to cause a health hazard.

As-is condition: Property in its existing condition.

Assessment: The imposition of a tax, charge, or levy, usually according to established rates.

Attorney in fact: An individual who is authorized to perform certain acts for another under a power of attorney.

Attorney's opinion of title: An abstract of title that an attorney has examined and has certified to be, in his or her opinion, an accurate statement of the facts concerning the property ownership.

Backup offer: A secondary bid for a property that the seller will accept if the first offer fails.

Bargain sale: The sale of a piece of property for less than market value.

Bargain and sale deed: A deed that carries with it no warranties against liens or other encumbrances, but that does imply that the grantor has the right to convey title.

Base line: The main imaginary line running east and west and crossing a principal meridian at a definite point, used by surveyors for reference in locating and describing land under the rectangular (government) survey system of legal description.

Basement: The area of a home below ground level.

Beneficiary: The lender who makes a loan, also called a mortgagee.

Bequest personal: Property given to a person through a will.

Bilateral contract: A contract in which both parties have reciprocal obligations toward each other.

Binder: Report issued by a title insurance company that details the condition of a home's title and provides guidelines for a title insurance policy.

Bond: An agreement that insures one party against loss by acts or defaults of another.

Boundary: The dividing line between two adjacent properties.

Breach of Contract: Violation of any of the terms or conditions of a contract; default; non-performance.

Broker: A licensed person who negotiates the purchase and sale of real estate.

Brokerage: The act of bringing together two or more parties in exchange for a fee or commission.

Builder upgrades: Extra house features or better finishing materials that a house builder offers.

Building code: Set of regulations that controls the construction or remodeling of residential houses and other structures.

Building inspector: A city or county employee who enforces the building code and ensures that work is correctly performed.

Building permit: A document issued by a local government agency that allows the construction or renovation of a house.

Bundle of rights: Ownership concept in real estate which embraces the rights of possession, use, enjoyment, and disposition.

Buyer–agency agreement: A buyer-agent relationship in which the broker is the agent for the buyer with fiduciary responsibilities to the buyer. The broker represents the buyer under the law of agency.

Buyer broker or agent: A real estate broker or agent who exclusively represents the buyer's interests in a transaction and whose commission, if agreed, is paid by the buyer rather than the seller.

Capital gains: Profit that an individual makes from the sale of real estate or investments.

Carport: A roof that covers a driveway or other parking area.

CC&R's: Covenants, conditions, and restrictions.

Chain of title: A sequential history of the conveyances, encumbrances, and records of ownership to a piece of property through the years from the original grant to present; the succession of owners as revealed through the public records.

Closing: The time when a transaction is consummated or the actual signing over of the documents and delivery of the deed; the time after signing when the documents are recorded.

Closing statement: A statement of settlement made by a broker or an escrow company that reflects the financial position of the buyer or seller in that particular real estate transaction.

Cloud on title: Any conditions revealed by a title search which may affect or impair the owner's title to property because of their apparent or probable validity.

Commission: An agent's compensation for performance of the duties of his agency; in real estate practice, a percentage of the selling price of the property or percentage of rentals.

Common element: In a condominium, land and all parts of a building normally used by all of the owners for their mutual convenience or safety.

Common interest: The percentage of undivided interest in the common elements of a building appertaining to each apartment in a condominium.

Community property: Property accumulated and owned in common through joint efforts of husband and wife during their marriage.

Condemnation: The process by which property of a private owner is taken for public use with a fair compensation of the owner under the right of eminent domain.

Condominium: Individual outright ownership of a single unit in a multi-unit property together with an interest in the common elements of that property.

Consideration: Valuable consideration, a promise or an act of legal value bargained for and received in return for a promise; good consideration.

Contingent: Dependent upon an uncertain future event.

Contract: A legal agreement between competent parties for a consideration to perform or refrain from performing certain acts.

Conveyance: The transfer of the title of land from one to another; an instrument which carries from one person to another an interest to property.

Clear title: A property that does not have liens, defects, or other legal encumbrances.

Cooperating broker: A broker who joins with another broker in the sale of real property, usually, one who represents the buyer of property listed with another broker, the selling broker.

Covenant: An agreement written into deeds and other instruments which promises or guarantees that something shall or shall not be done; an agreement stipulating certain uses or nonuses of property.

Damages: The indemnity recoverable by an injured party to compensate him for the loss suffered through an act of default of another.

Deed: An instrument in writing, duly executed and delivered by the grantor, that conveys to the grantee some right or interest in or to real estate.

Deed Tax: Tax paid by seller upon transfer of deed.

Delivery: The act or intent of transferring an instrument from one person to another in such a way that it cannot be recalled.

Depreciation: Loss of value due to physical deterioration or functional or economic obsolescence.

Deterioration: Loss in value due to wear and tear.

Direct sales comparison approach: A means of estimating value by comparing recent sales of comparable properties to the subject property after making appropriate adjustments for any differences.

Earnest money: Initial payment made by a purchaser of real estate as evidence of good faith.

Easement: A right, privilege, or interest which one party has in the land of another.

Easement in gross: An easement which encumbers the land, and is usually given to a quasi-public corporation, such as an electric or telephone company.

Easement by prescription: A method of acquiring a right to a portion of property by lapse of time, in the manner of adverse possession.

Eminent domain: The right of a government to take private property for public use upon the payment of fair compensation.

Encroachment: A building or fixture which intrudes partly or wholly upon the property of another.

Equity: The interest or value which an owner has in real estate over and above the debts against it.

Escalation clause: A clause in a contract permitting an adjustment of certain payments up or down to cover certain contingencies; mostly found in agreements of sale, mortgages, and leases.

Escrow: The deposit of instruments and funds with instructions to a third neutral party to carry out the provisions of an agreement of contract.

Exchange: A method of conveying real property by trading with another property.

Exclusive right to sell: A written agreement between owner and agent giving agent the right to collect a commission if the property is sold by anyone during the term of his agreement.

Execute: To complete, to perform, to make, to do, to follow out; to execute a deed, to make a deed, including especially signing; to execute a contract, to perform the contract, to follow out to the end, to complete.

Executed contract: A contract that is fully performed.

External obsolescence: Loss in value due to factors outside of the property (such as nearby airport).

Federal Housing Administration (FHA): An agency of the federal government which insures certain real estate loans.

First refusal, right of: A right, usually given by an owner to a lessee, which gives the lessee the first chance to buy the property if the owner decides to sell. The owner must have a legitimate offer which the lessee can then match or refuse.

Fixture: An article of personal property which has been installed in or attached to land or a building thereon in such a manner that it is now considered to be a part of the real estate.

General lien: A lien which attaches to all property owned by the debtor.

Grant: A transfer of real property.

Grantee: The purchaser; the person to whom an interest in realty is conveyed.

Grantor: The seller; the person who conveys an interest in realty by deed.

Ground lease: A lease for the use of the land, usually providing for improvements to be placed on the land by the user.

Heir: One who succeeds to the estate, descendant.

Holding escrow: An arrangement whereby escrow holds the final title documents pursuant to an agreement of sale.

Holdover tenant: A tenant who remains in possession of a property after expiration of lease term.

Homestead: A right given to a home owner or head of family to designate real estate as his homestead, and said homestead is exempt up to a stated amount from execution by his creditors; a tract of land whose ownership has been established under the provisions of the Homestead Act.

Improvements: All real estate except land. Includes buildings, fixtures, fences, curbs, and sewers.

Incapacity: The lack of legal qualifications making a person incapable of performing some act. Mental deficients and minors, lack capacity to perform certain acts.

Instrument: A written legal document.

Intestate: A person who dies without a will or with one that is defective in form.

Involuntary lien: A lien imposed against property without consent of an owner: e.g., taxes, special assessments and federal income tax liens.

Joint tenancy: Ownership by two or more persons with rights of survivorship; all joint tenants own equal interests and have equal rights in the property; each owner is possessed of an undivided part of the whole.

Joint venture: A joining of two or more people in a specific business enterprise; similar to a partnership but generally with no intention of a continuing relationship beyond the original purpose.

Judgment: The final determination of the rights and liabilities of the parties by a court in an action before it.

Market value: The highest price a ready, willing, and able buyer, not forced to buy, will pay to a ready, willing, and able seller, not forced to sell, allowing a reasonable time for exposure in the open market.

Mechanic's lien: A lien which exists against real property in favor of persons who have performed work or furnished materials for the improvement of real estate.

Misrepresentation: A false statement of a material fact made with the intent to induce some action by another party.

Multiple Listing Service (M.L.S.): An arrangement among brokers whereby they share their listings.

NAR: The National Association of REALTORS. Only brokers who are members of local real estate boards are entitled to use the trademark name "Realtor." Salespeople are called "Realtor-Associates."

Personal property: Any property not real property.

Power of attorney: A written instrument authorizing a person (an attorney in fact) to act as the agent on behalf of another to the extent indicated in the instrument.

Probate: An action of the court to determine the validity and legality of a last will and testament.

Procuring cause: The cause of a series of events which leads to the consummation of a sale.

Prorate: To divide or distribute proportionately; to divide monies, usually at time of closing, proportionately between seller and buyer.

PUD: Planned Unit Development. A planned combination of diverse land uses, such as housing, recreation, and shopping, in one contained development or subdivision.

Quiet enjoyment: The right of an owner or tenant legally in possession to the use of property without interference from the landlord or grantor, or anyone claiming through him.

Quiet title: A court action brought to establish title or to remove a cloud on the title; an action clearing tax titles or titles based upon adverse possession.

Quitclaim deed: A deed containing no warranties or covenants, which relinquishes any interest, title, or claim to property the grantor may have, if any.

Realtor: A broker who belongs to NAR. (See NAR).

Realtor associate: A salesperson who works for a realtor and belongs to the local Board of Realtors.

Re-conveyance: A conveyance to the land owner of the title held by a trustee under a deed of trust.

Recording: The act of writing or entering an instrument into a book of public records, which constitutes notice to all persons of the rights or claims contained in the instrument.

Remainder estate: An estate created by single grant simultaneously with another which vests with a third party after termination of the prior estate, such as a life state.

Rescind: To annul; cancel.

Rescission: The annulling, revocation, or repealing of a contract by mutual consent of the parties, or for cause by either party to the contract, and returning the parties to their original position (the "status quo").

Restriction: A clause in a deed or other written instrument limiting the use to which the property may be put.

Setback: An ordinance prohibiting the erection of a building or structure between the curb or other established line and the setback line; the distance a house must be set back from the street in accordance with local zoning rules.

Severalty: Sole or independent ownership.

Simple interest: Interest computed upon the declining balance of a particular amount; as principal declines so does the interest payment.

Special assessment: An assessment generally made against only those specific parcels of realty directly benefiting there from.

Specific performance: A remedy which the court will grant in certain cases, compelling the defendant to perform or carry out the terms of a valid, existing agreement or contract.

Tax deed: A deed for property sold by a government unit for nonpayment of taxes.

Tax sale: A sale of property usually at auction for non-payment of assessed taxes.

Tenancy by the entirety: A tenancy held by husband and wife giving each the equal right to possession and enjoyment during their joint lives, along with the right to sole ownership upon the death of either partner.

Survey: The process by which a parcel of land is measured and its area ascertained.

Undivided interest: Title to property owned by two or more persons, none of whom is entitled to claim or possess any specific part.

Unilateral contract: A contract whereby only one party is obligated to perform his obligation to another.

Unmarketable title: A title containing substantial defects which might cause a prospective purchaser to suffer title litigation and possible loss.

Variance: Permission obtained form zoning authorities permitting the construction of a building or structure that is forbidden by present zoning ordinances; a departure from the current zoning regulation.

Vested interest: A present right or title to realty, but with possession delayed to some uncertain time in the future.

Refinancing may be a good option to lower monthly payments or get cash out of the home equity.

B

MORTGAGE GLOSSARY

Additional principal payment: Extra money included in the monthly payment to help reduce the principal balance and to shorten the term of the loan.

Add-on interest: The interest a borrower pays on the principal for the duration on the loan.

Adjustable rate mortgage (ARM): A loan with an interest rate that is periodically adjusted to reflect changes in a specified financial index and with a margin.

Adjustment period: The amount of time between interest rate adjustments in an adjustable rate mortgage.

Alienation clause: A provision that requires the borrower to pay the balance of the loan in a lump sum after the property is sold or transferred.

Alternative mortgage: Any home loan that does not conform to a standard fixed-rate mortgage.

Amortization: The process of paying the principal and interest on a loan through scheduled installments.

Amortization table: Mathematical chart that shows the monthly or yearly interest and principal over the period of the loan.

Annual mortgagor statement: A yearly statement to borrowers that details the remaining principal and amounts paid for taxes and interest.

Annual percentage rate (APR): The cost of the loan expressed as a yearly rate on the loan balance.

Anticipatory breach: A communication that informs a party that the obligations of the original contract will not be fulfilled.

Application fee: The fee that lenders charge to process a loan application.

Assumption of mortgage: Taking title to property by assuming liability for payment of an existing note secured by a mortgage.

Assumption clause: A provision that allows a buyer to take responsibility for the mortgage from a seller.

Assumption fee: A fee the lender charges to process new records for a buyer who assumes an existing loan.

Balloon loan: A mortgage in which monthly installments are not large enough to repay the loan by the end of the term, in consequence, the final payment is the remainder of the principal.

Balloon payment: Is the final installment payment on a note which is greater than the preceding installment payments and pays the loan in full.

Bankruptcy: A condition of financial insolvency in which a person's liabilities exceed his assets.

Bi-weekly mortgage: A mortgage loan that requires payments every two weeks and helps repay the loan over a shorter time.

Blanket mortgage: One mortgage covering two or more specific properties owned by one owner.

Buy-down: The one-time, nonrefundable prepayment of a portion of the interest of a loan to subsidize reduced monthly payments calculated with a reduced effective interest rate.

Call option: A clause in a loan agreement that allows a lender to require the unpaid balance at any time.

Cap: A limit on the amount the interest rate can increase in an adjustable rate mortgage.

Deed of trust: Similar to a mortgage but title is transferred to a trustee pending payment of the debt.

Deficiency judgment: A judgment for the balance of a debt; issued when the net proceeds from the foreclosure sale are less than the indebtedness sued upon.

Discount points: A unit of measurement used for various loans charges; one point equals 1 percent of the amount of the loan.

Down payment: The amount of cash paid by a buyer which, added to the mortgage amount, equals the total sales price. At the time of closing this is referred to as equity.

Due on sale: A mortgage clause permitting acceleration of the loan if the mortgagor attempts to transfer title or interest to the secured property.

Estate: The degree, quantity, nature, and extent of interest a person has in real property.

Fannie Mae (Federal National Mortgage Association): An agency formerly of the federal government that buys and sells mortgages in the secondary money market.

Freddie Mac (Federal Home Loan Mortgage Corporation): A corporation established to purchase primarily conventional mortgage loans in the secondary mortgage market.

Fee simple: An estate in real property by which the owner has the greatest power over the title that it is possible to have, being an absolute estate; an estate of inheritance belonging to the owner, that he may dispose of, trade, or will, as he chooses.

Fiduciary: A person in a position of great trust and confidence, as the relationship between principal and broker.

Foreclosure: Procedure whereby property pledged as security for a debt is sold to pay the debt in event of default in payments or terms.

Fraud: The intentional and successful employment of deception in order to cheat or deceive another person and to gain some dishonest advantage.

Graduated mortgage: One where monthly payments start low and increase later. An FHA245 is one of these.

Ginnie Mae (Government National Mortgage Association): Government agency that plays an important role in the secondary mortgage market. It sells mortgage-backed securities that are backed by pools of FHA and VA loans.

General warranty: A deed in which the grantor fully warrants good clear title to the premises. Used in most real estate deed transfers, a general warranty deed offers the greatest protection of any deed.

Gross income: Total income derived from a business or income property before expenses are deducted.

Hypothecate: To place property as security; to mortgage.

Impounds: A reserve account often required by lenders to cover future payments of taxes, lease rent, and insurance.

Installment contract: A contract which provides for payment of a purchase price in installments; an agreement of sale. Also called installment land contract or installment sale.

Interim financing: A short-term loan obtained to cover financing of the construction of a building.

Junior lien: A subordinate lien.

Junior mortgage: A mortgage which is subordinate to prior existing mortgage on the same realty.

Marketable title: Title free and clear of objectionable liens or encumbrances; title which is free from reasonable doubts or defects, which can be readily sold or mortgaged.

Mortgage: An instrument in writing which, when recorded, creates a lien upon property pledged as security for the repayment of a debt or obligation.

Mortgage banker: A corporation or firm which makes delivers and services mortgage loans.

Mortgage broker: A person or firm which acts as an intermediary between borrower and lender.

Mortgagee: The party who lends money and accepts a mortgage to secure the payment of the debt.

Mortgagor: The party who borrows money and gives a mortgage on the property as security for his obligation to repay the debt.

Negotiable instrument: A written instrument signed by its maker or drawer, containing an unconditional promise to pay a certain sum of money; can be passed freely from one person to another.

Negotiate: To transact business; to arrange terms of a contract.

Net income: With reference to property, the sum derived after a vacancy allowance and expenses have been deducted from the gross income; generally described as net income before depreciation, and usually defining the income a property will earn in a normal year's operation (net operating income).

Nominal consideration: One bearing no relation to the real value of the contract. An example is a property which is deeded for $10.00.

Nonconforming use: A use which is contrary to zoning laws, but which is permitted because the use was allowed before the zoning law came into effect; a grandfather clause.

Note: A written instrument acknowledging a debt and promising payment.

Obsolescence: Functional obsolescence or lack of desirability in terms of layout, style, and design as compared with that of a new property serving the same function; economic obsolescence or a loss in value from causes in the neighborhood but outside the property itself.

Ordinance: A legislative enactment of a city or county, such as zoning.

Over improvement: An improvement which is not the highest and best use for the site on which it is placed, usually by reason of excess size or cost.

Package mortgage: A mortgage commonly used in subdivision developments whereby chattels such as appliances are "packaged" into the mortgage along with the real property.

Partnership: A contract between two or more persons to carry on as co-owners of a business, and to share the profits in certain proportions.

Power of sale: A provision in a mortgage permitting the lender, upon borrower's default, to sell the secured property at public auction without need to have a court foreclose.

Prepayment clause: The clause in a mortgage or note stating the penalty, if any, for payment before it actually becomes due.

Prescription: An easement or title obtained by possession for a prescribed period; prescriptive rights.

Primary money market: The source of loan funds available directly to borrowers, whether for first or second mortgages; loan originations.

Prime rate: The minimum interest rate charged by a bank on short-term loans to its best clients.

Principal: A sum of money owed as a debt upon which interest is calculated.

Purchase money mortgage: A mortgage on property given by a buyer, either to the seller or to a third party, to secure a portion of the purchase price.

Refinance: To obtain a new loan to pay off an existing mortgage or agreement of sale.

Release: The relinquishment or surrender of a right, claim, or interest.

Release of mortgage: The instrument given by the mortgagee to the mortgagor indicating discharge of the mortgage.

Rider: An addition, addendum, or endorsement annexed to a document; it should be signed or initialed.

Right of way: An easement or right of passage over another's land.

Sale and leaseback: The sale and subsequent leasing back by the seller-lessee.

Second mortgage: One that is recorded after a first mortgage, thus second in priority.

Statute of limitations: Laws setting forth the period of time in which suit can be brought for a particular act.

Subordination clause: A clause in a mortgage or lease stating that the rights of the holder shall be secondary or subordinate to a subsequent encumbrance.

Take-out financing: Permanent or long-term financing of individual condominium units for their respective buyers.

Title: Evidence that an owner of land is in lawful possession thereof; ownership.

Title insurance: A policy of insurance which indemnifies the holder for loss sustained by reason of a defect in the title provided the loss does not result from a defect excluded by the policy provisions.

Trust deed: A deed given by borrower to trustee to be held pending fulfillment of an obligation.

Trustee: One who holds property in trust for another to secure the performance of an obligation.

Truth-in-lending: A federal law letting borrowers know the exact cost of obtaining credit; a disclosure document.

Upset price: The minimum price at a foreclosure sale below which the property cannot be sold.

Usury charging: A rate of interest on a loan greater that that permitted by law. It is presently 12 percent on personal loans.

Valid: Having binding force; legally sufficient and authorized by law.

Valuation: The estimated worth of property.

Variable Rate Mortgage: Mortgage in which interest rate will fluctuate depending on term of mortgage.

Veterans Administration (VA). Also, Department of Veterans Affairs (DVA): An agency of the federal government whose activities include guaranteed repayment of certain loans in the event of default.

Void: To have no force or effect; that which is unenforceable.

Voluntary Lien: Any lien placed on property with consent of, or as a result of, the voluntary act of the owner, i.e., a mortgage.

Waive: To relinquish or abandon; the abandonment of some claim or right.

Warranty deed: A deed in which the grantor fully warrants a good clear title to the property; a deed that contains covenants title.

Wrap-around mortgage: Method of financing in which a new mortgage is placed in a secondary position; an all–inclusive mortgage.

Writ of execution: A writ or court order authorizing and directing an officer of the court to carry out the judgment or decree of the court.

Zone: An area set aside for specific use, subject to certain restrictions or restraints; also part of tax map description.

Zoning: An act of the city or county authorities by exercise of police power in regulating, controlling, or specifying the type of use to which the property may be put in specific areas.

C

CONTRACTS AND FORMS

This appendix contains worksheets, forms, and sample contracts:

The contracts are for review and informational purposes only. Most states have specific purchasing regulations and you will need the assistance of a qualified real estate attorney to review and/or prepare specific contracts.

All the contracts and forms in Appendix C can also be found on the companion CD-ROM.

BUDGET WORKSHEET

Before you begin house hunting you will want to estimate your monthly income and expenses. This worksheet will help you itemize costs and determine expenses. You may also want to use an online mortgage calculator to figure interest rate and loan terms. See **www.mortgage-calc.com** or **www.bankrate.com/brm/mortgage-calculator.asp** for a number of different options.

MONTHLY INCOME	
Wages & Salary (after taxes)	$ _____
Interest Income	$ _____
Investment Income	$ _____
Other Income	$ _____
TOTAL MONTHLY INCOME:	$ _____

HOUSING EXPENSES	
Mortgage	$ _____
Property Taxes	$ _____
Home Repairs/Maintenance/HOA Dues	$ _____
TOTAL HOUSING EXPENSES:	$ _____

DEBT EXPENSES	
Credit Cards	$ _____
Student Loans	$ _____
Other Loans	$ _____
TOTAL DEBT EXPENSES:	$ _____

UTILITY EXPENSES

Electricity $ _____

Water and Sewer $ _____

Natural Gas or Fuel $ _____

Telephone $ _____

Cell Phone $ _____

TOTAL UTILITY EXPENSES: $ _____

AUTO/TRANSPORTATION EXPENSES

Auto Payment $ _____

Gasoline/Oil $ _____

Auto Repairs/Maintenance/Fees $ _____

Other Transportation (tolls, bus, taxis) $ _____

TOTAL TRANSPORT EXPENSES: $ _____

INSURANCE EXPENSES

Homeowners Insurance $ _____

Health Insurance $ _____

Life Insurance $ _____

Auto Insurance $ _____

Other $ _____

TOTAL INSURANCE EXPENSES: $ _____

PERSONAL/MEDICAL EXPENSES

Child Support $ _____

Alimony $ _____

Child Care $ _____

Unreimbursed Medical, Copays $ _____

Personal Fitness (gym, etc) $ _____

Other $ _____

Other $ _____

Other $ _____

TOTAL PERSONAL EXPENSES: $ _____

INVESTMENTS AND SAVINGS

401(K) or IRA $ _____

Stocks/Bonds/Mutual Funds $ _____

College Fund $ _____

Savings $ _____

Emergency Fund $ _____

Other $ _____

TOTAL INVESTMENT EXPENSES: $ _____

FOOD EXPENSES

Groceries $ _____

Dining Out $ _____

Other (snacks. lunches, etc) $ _____

TOTAL FOOD EXPENSES: $ _____

ENTERTAINMENT/RECREATION/MISC

Cable TV $ _____

Internet $ _____

Videos/Movies $ _____

Computer Expense $ _____

Hobbies $ _____

Subscriptions and Dues $ _____

Vacation $ _____

Pet Food $ _____

Pet Grooming, Boarding, Vet $ _____

Clothing $ _____

Toiletries, Household Products $ _____

Gifts/Donations $ _____

Grooming (Hair, Make-up, Other) $ _____

Other _____ $ _____

Other _____ $ _____

Other _____ $ _____

Other _____ $ _____

Other _____ $ _____

Other _____ $ _____

Other _____ $ _____

Other _____ $ _____

TOTAL MISC EXPENSES: $ _____

INCOME AND EXPENSE SUMMARY

TOTAL INCOME (subtract) $ _____

    Total Housing Expenses $ _____

    Total Debt Expenses $ _____

    Total Utility Expenses $ _____

    Total Transportation Expenses $ _____

    Total Insurance Expenses $ _____

    Total Personal/Medical Expenses $ _____

    Total Investment Expenses $ _____

    Total Food Expenses $ _____

    Total Entertainment Expenses $ _____

TOTAL EXPENSES $ _____

AMOUNT OVER/UNDER BUDGET: $ _____

HOME FEATURES WORKSHEET

Once you have determined your budget, it is a good idea to identify the features you are looking for in a home. Compare your ideal features to listings to determine which homes you want to view. You can also share this list with an agent to help him or her meet your needs.

1. The house I am interested in purchasing is:
    ❏ New
    ❏ Existing home, from _____ to _____ years old.
    ❏ Historic home
    ❏ Custom built

2. My price range is from _____ to _____.

3. The home's condition should be:
    ❏ Excellent, ready to move-in
    ❏ Good, minor remodeling acceptable
    ❏ Fixer-upper

4. The type of home I am interested in (check all that apply):
    ❏ Ranch   ❏ Split-level   ❏ 2-Story
    ❏ Traditional   ❏ Vintage   ❏ Modern
    ❏ Cape Cod   ❏ Duplex   ❏ Condo/Townhouse
    ❏ Other _____

5. The type of exterior I am interested in is:
    ❏ Brick   ❏ Siding   ❏ Stucco
    ❏ Wood   ❏ Other _____

6. The number of bedrooms I would like is _____.

7. The number of bathrooms I would like is_____.

8. Rate the following features by order of importance with 1 being very important and 5 being not important.

Garage Attached Detached	1	2	3	4	5
Garage Size (cars 1 2 3)	1	2	3	4	5
Carport	1	2	3	4	5
Private driveway	1	2	3	4	5
Privacy from neighbors	1	2	3	4	5
Master bedroom	1	2	3	4	5
Ground floor bathroom	1	2	3	4	5
Eat-in kitchen	1	2	3	4	5
Formal dining room	1	2	3	4	5
Separate family room	1	2	3	4	5
Home office	1	2	3	4	5
Fireplace	1	2	3	4	5
Central air conditioning	1	2	3	4	5
Basement	1	2	3	4	5
Attic	1	2	3	4	5
Deck	1	2	3	4	5
Patio	1	2	3	4	5
Landscaping	1	2	3	4	5
Security system	1	2	3	4	5
Pool	1	2	3	4	5
Laundry room	1	2	3	4	5
Mudroom	1	2	3	4	5
Dishwasher	1	2	3	4	5
Garbage disposal	1	2	3	4	5
Pantry	1	2	3	4	5
Skylights	1	2	3	4	5
Walk-in closets	1	2	3	4	5
Wall-to-wall carpeting	1	2	3	4	5
Hardwood floors	1	2	3	4	5
Ceiling fans	1	2	3	4	5

Tile floors	1	2	3	4	5
Additional closets/storage	1	2	3	4	5
Hot tub	1	2	3	4	5
Large front yard	1	2	3	4	5
Large backyard	1	2	3	4	5
Minimum exterior upkeep	1	2	3	4	5

Other important features not listed: _____

_____

_____

_____

9. Rate the desired location by order of importance with 1 being very important and 5 being not important. Close to:

Place of employment	1	2	3	4	5
Spouse's place of employment	1	2	3	4	5
Schools	1	2	3	4	5
Shopping	1	2	3	4	5
Parks/playgrounds	1	2	3	4	5
Recreation facilities	1	2	3	4	5
Places of worship	1	2	3	4	5
Access to transportation	1	2	3	4	5
Proximity to shopping	1	2	3	4	5
Community services	1	2	3	4	5
Recreation center	1	2	3	4	5

Additional Notes:

_____

_____

_____

_____

_____

_____

REAL ESTATE AGENT QUESTIONNAIRE

If you decide to work with a real estate agent, it is a good idea to interview him or her. Don't be afraid to ask questions to make sure you have a good match and ally in finding your first home. The following basic questions are an essential start.

1. How long have you been a real estate agent? How long has your firm been in business?

2. Can I see your references?

3. What process and tools do you employ to help me search for my new home?

4. How many homes will I likely see before I find a home I want to buy?

5. Will I be competing against other buyers?

6. How do you handle multiple offers?

7. How will my offer be presented to the seller? Do you present offers yourself?

8. What is your average list-price-to-sales-price ratio?
   A good buyer's agent should be able to negotiate a final price lower than list price. Buyer's agent ratios should be below 95%, as his or her goal is to get you the best price.

9. Why should I choose you? Can you tell me a few ways you stand out from other agents?

10. I would like to review all documents in advance before I sign then and have them reviewed by my attorney. Will this be a problem?
You should be provided sample copies of copies of the Buyer's Broker Agreement, Agency Disclosures, Purchase Agreement, and Buyer Disclosures.

11. Can you refer me to other professionals such as mortgage brokers, home inspectors, and title companies?
You should be given a written list with more than one option for each service. If you see the term "affiliated" it could mean that the agent or company receives compensation for referrals, so be sure to ask if that is the case.

12. How much do you charge?
Remember, real estate fees are negotiable. Agents usually receive a percentage (typically 1 to 5 percent) to represent one side of a transaction.

13. If I am unhappy with your services, can I cancel the agreement at any time? What is your company policy regarding canceled agreements?

14 Are there any other issues I need to know about?
Your agent should make you feel comfortable and be willing to listen to your preferences in housing. This last question is a good opportunity to make sure he or she is forthcoming and ready to take time to talk to you.

HOME EVALUATION CHECKLIST

Each time you look at a property, take this checklist along to review the merits. Fill it out for each house you are interested in. It will help you assess the costs, location, and overall condition to compare properties.

PROPERTY

Property Address: _____

_____

_____

Asking Price: _____

Real Estate Taxes: _____

Lot Size/Acreage: _____

Age of House: _____

Style of House/Number of Stories: _____

Initial Impression: _____

_____

_____

_____

_____

_____

_____

_____

_____

_____

UTILITIES

Estimated Water Bill: _____

Estimated Electric Bill: _____

Estimated Heating Bill: _____

Estimated Cooling Bill: _____

Other: _____

_____

NEIGHBORHOOD

Streets Maintained: ❏ Yes   ❏ No

Neighboring Houses
Maintained: ❏ Yes   ❏ No

Sidewalks: ❏ Yes   ❏ No

Street Lights: ❏ Yes   ❏ No

Streets Maintained: ❏ Yes   ❏ No

Low Traffic Volume: ❏ Yes   ❏ No

Low Overall Noise: ❏ Yes   ❏ No

Garbage Collection: ❏ Yes   ❏ No

Restrictions:

_____

_____

_____

_____

LOCATION

Check all that apply:

Close to:

❏ Transportation   ❏ Schools
❏ Grocery Store   ❏ Shopping Center
❏ Expressways   ❏ Doctors
❏ Dentists   ❏ Hospital/Medical Center
❏ Trains   ❏ Airport
❏ Industry   ❏ Entertainment
❏ Parks   ❏ Playgrounds

Location Pros (list:)

_____

_____

_____

_____

_____

_____

_____

Location Cons (list:)

_____

_____

_____

_____

_____

_____

EXTERIOR CONDITION

Type of Exterior:

❏ Brick   ❏ Stucco

❏ Siding (list type) _____

❏ Other (list type) _____

Rate Exterior Appearance:

Overall Exterior:	❏ Good	❏ Fair	❏ Poor
Roof Condition:	❏ Good	❏ Fair	❏ Poor
Foundation Condition:	❏ Good	❏ Fair	❏ Poor
Driveway:	❏ Good	❏ Fair	❏ Poor
Garage:	❏ Good	❏ Fair	❏ Poor
Patio:	❏ Good	❏ Fair	❏ Poor
Yard:	❏ Good	❏ Fair	❏ Poor
Landscaping:	❏ Good	❏ Fair	❏ Poor
Fencing:	❏ Good	❏ Fair	❏ Poor
Security:	❏ Good	❏ Fair	❏ Poor
Windows:	❏ Good	❏ Fair	❏ Poor

Other (list):

_____

_____

_____

_____

_____

INTERIOR

Number of Bedrooms: _____

Do bedrooms have closets?   ❏ Yes   ❏ No

Number of Bathrooms: _____

Dining Room:	❏ Yes	❏ No
Eat-In Kitchen:	❏ Yes	❏ No
Family Room/Den:	❏ Yes	❏ No
Additional Closets:	❏ Yes	❏ No
Laundry Room:	❏ Yes	❏ No
Adequate Storage:	❏ Yes	❏ No
Attic:	❏ Yes	❏ No
Finished Basement:	❏ Yes	❏ No
Room for Expansion:	❏ Yes	❏ No
Fireplace:	❏ Yes	❏ No
Carpeting:	❏ Yes	❏ No

List any areas/items that need remodeling: _____

_____

_____

_____

_____

_____

_____

APPLIANCES

Check any appliances that are included:

Washer:	❏ Yes	❏ No
Dryer:	❏ Yes	❏ No
Refrigerator:	❏ Yes	❏ No
Freezer:	❏ Yes	❏ No
Stove/Oven:	❏ Yes	❏ No
Garbage Disposal:	❏ Yes	❏ No
Dishwasher:	❏ Yes	❏ No

Other (list):

_____

_____

SYSTEMS

Type of Heat:_____

Age of Heating System: _____

Central Air Conditioning: _____

Type of Water Heater: _____

Age of Water Heater: _____

Capacity of Water Heater: _____

Insulation: _____

Electrical Condition: _____

Plumbing System Condition: _____

Sewer/septic System: _____

RESIDENTIAL PURCHASE AGREEMENT
(Joint Escrow Instructions and Earnest Money Receipt)

Buyer's Broker:_____	Agent's Name: _____
Company: _____	E-mail: _____
Address: _____	
License #:_____	Fax: _____
MLS Public ID#: _____	Phone: _____
Seller's Broker: _____	Agent's Name: _____
Company: _____	E-mail: _____
Address: _____	
License #: _____	Fax: _____
MLS Public ID#: _____	Phone: _____

On this day of _____, 20 _____, ("Buyer"), _____
_____(hereby offers to purchase) _____
_____ ("Property"), _____
_____, County of _____, State of _____ for the purchase
price of $ _____ ("Purchase Price") on the following terms and conditions:

1. FINANCING TERMS

$ _____   A. **EARNEST MONEY OR DEPOSIT IS** ☐ presented with this offer - OR - ☐ _____
_____

$ _____   B. **ADDITIONAL DEPOSIT** will be placed in escrow within _____ days after acceptance.

$ _____   C. **BALANCE OF CASH PAYMENT** (Balance of Down Payment) in cash or certified funds to
be paid at Close of Escrow ("COE").

$ _____   D. **NEW FIRST LOAN:**
_____
_____
_____
_____

$ _____   E. ☐ **EXISTING FINANCING:** ☐ Assumption of, ☐ Subject to existing loan of record described
as follows: _____

$ _____   F. ☐ **SELLER FINANCING:** ☐ First Loan, ☐ Second Loan, ☐ Third Loan, secured by the pro-
erty. ☐ Seller Financing Addendum is attached and made part of this Agreement.

$ _____   G. **TOTAL PURCHASE PRICE.** (NOT include closing costs.)

**Each party acknowledges that he/she has read, understood, and agrees to each and every provision of this page
unless a particular paragraph is otherwise modified by addendum or counteroffer.**

BUYER(S) INITIALS _____/_____   SELLER(S) INITIALS _____/_____

2. NEW LOAN APPLICATION: Buyer agrees to sulma copleted loan application with the reqired inforation for loan qualification with a lender within _____ business days of Seller's acceptance of this offer. Buyer agrees to use efforts to obtain financing under the terms and conditions outlined in this Agreement. Buyer ☐ will - OR - ☐ will not authorize lender to provide loan status updates to Seller's and Buyer's Brokers, as well as Escrow Officer.

3. SALE OF OTHER PROPERTY : This Agreement is contingent upon the sale (and closing) of another property:

_____

_____

_____

Said Property ☐ is not - OR - ☐ is presently in escrow with _____
☐   This Agreement is NOT contingent upon the sale (and closing) of another property.

4. ESCROW:

  A. OPENING OF ESCROW: The purchase of the Property shall be consummated through Escrow ("Escrow"). Opening of Escrow shall take place by the end of one (1) business day after execution of this Agreement ("Opening of Escrow"), at

_____

_____

_____

  B. EARNEST MONEY: Upon Seller and Buyer signing this Agreement and all counteroffers or addenda, Buyer's earnest money shall be deposited per the following:

_____

_____

  C. CLOSE OF ESCROW: Close of Escrow ("COE") shall be on (date) _____ .

5. PRORATIONS, FEES, AND EXPENSES:

  A. TITLE , ESCROW FEES, and PRORATIONS: (Such as Escrow Fees, Lender's Title Policy, Owner's Title Policy, Real
    Property Transfer Tax, Fees and Assessments):

PAID BY SELLER:

_____

_____

PAID BY BUYER:

_____

_____

OTHER:

_____

_____

All prorations will be based on a 30-day month and will be calculated as of COE. Prorations will be based upon figures available at closing. Any supplementals or adjustments that occur after COE will be handled by the parties outside of Escrow.

  **Each party acknowledges that he/she has read, understood, and agrees to each and every provision of this page
  unless a particular paragraph is otherwise modified by addendum or counteroffer.**

  BUYER(S) INITIALS _____/_____   SELLER(S) INITIALS _____/_____

C. INSPECTIONS OF PHYSICAL CONDITION OF THE PROPERTY: Buyer will have the right to retain, at his/her expense licensed experts to examine the property. Experts may include, but are not limited to architects, engineers, contractors, surveyors, and structural pest control operators. Said experts may inspect the property for any structural and nonstructrual conditions including: roofing, electrical, plumbing, heating cooling, appliances, pool/hot tub, well, septic system, boundaries, and environmental hazards such as toxic substances, asbestos, mold, radon gas, and lead-based paint. If requested by the Seller in writing, Buyer will furnish written copies of all inspection reports obtained at no cost to Seller. Buyer will approve or disapprove in writing all inspection reports within _____ days after acceptance. In the event of Buyer's disapproval, Buyer may elect to terminate this agreement or invite Seller to negotiate repairs, within a time frame of _____ days.

D. MAINTENANCE: Until possession is delivered, Seller will maintain all structures, landscaping, and grounds in the same general condition as of the date of acceptance or physical condition, whichever is later. Seller agrees to deliver the property in a neat and clean condition with all debris and personal property removed.

E. PERSONAL PROPERTY: The following personal property will be transferred with the sale of the property with no real value unless stated otherwise herein. All existing electrical, mechanical, lighting, plumbing and heating fixtures, ceiling fans, fireplace inserts, gas logs and grates, solar systems, built-in appliances, window and door screens, awnings, shutters, window coverings, attached floor coverings, television antennas, satellite dishes, private integrated telephone systems, air coolers/conditioners, pool/spa equipment, garage door openers/remote controls, mailbox, in-ground landscaping, trees/shrubs, water softeners, water purifiers, security systems/alarms.

Unless itemized here, personal property is not included in the condition of the sale:_____
_____
_____
_____

F. LENDER'S FEES: Seller will contribute $ _____ to Buyer's Lender's Fees and Buyer's Title and Escrow Fees ☐ including - OR - ☐ excluding costs which Seller must pay pursuant to loan program requirements.

G. HOME PROTECTION PLAN: Buyer and Seller acknowledge that they have been made aware of Home Protection Plans that provide coverage to Buyer after COE. Buyer ☐ waives - OR - ☐ requires a Home Protection Plan with _____
_____.

Buyer will order the Home Protection Plan. ☐ Seller - OR - ☐ Buyer will pay for the Home Protection Plan at a price not to exceed $_____. Neither Seller nor Brokers make any representation as to the extent of coverage or deductibles of such plans. Escrow Holder is not responsible for ordering the Home Protection Plan.

H. OTHER FEES: Buyer will also pay $_____ to Buyer's Broker for_____
_____
_____
_____
_____
_____
_____
_____
_____
_____

Each party acknowledges that he/she has read, understood, and agrees to each and every provision of this page unless a particular paragraph is otherwise modified by addendum or counteroffer.

BUYER(S) INITIALS _____/_____   SELLER(S) INITIALS _____/_____

6. TITLE INSURANCE: Buyer will be provided with the following type of title insurance policy:_____

_____
_____
_____
_____
_____
_____

7. TRANSFER OF TITLE: Upon COE, Buyer shall tender to Seller the agreed upon purchase price, and Seller shall tender to Buyer marketable title to the Property free of all encumbrances other than (1) current pro-rata Property taxes, (2) covenants, conditions, and restrictions and related restrictions, (3) zoning or master plan restrictions and public utility easements; and (4) obligations assumed and encumbrances accepted by Buyer prior to COE.

8. DELIVERY OF POSESSION: Seller shall deliver the Property along with keys, alarm codes, and garage door opener/controls outside of Escrow, upon COE. In the event Seller does not vacate the Property by COE, Seller shall be considered a trespasser and shall be liable to Buyer for the sum of $ _____ per calendar day. Any personal property left on the Property after COE shall be considered abandoned by Seller.

The following personal property is included in the condition of the sale:_____

_____
_____
_____
_____
_____
_____
_____
_____
_____

9. DISCLOSURES: Within _____ days of Seller's acceptance of this Agreement, Seller will provide the following Disclosures (each of which is incorporated herein by this reference).

_____
_____
_____
_____
_____
_____
_____
_____
_____
_____
_____
_____
_____

Each party acknowledges that he/she has read, understood, and agrees to each and every provision of this page unless a particular paragraph is otherwise modified by addendum or counteroffer.

BUYER(S) INITIALS _____/_____   SELLER(S) INITIALS _____/_____

10. BUYER'S DUE DILIGENCE:

    A. DUE DILIGENCE PERIOD: Buyer shall have _____ calendar days from acceptance of this offer to complete Buyer's Due Diligence. During this period Buyer shall have the exclusive right at Buyer's discretion to cancel this Agreement. In the event of such cancellation, unless otherwise agreed herein, the EMD will be refunded to Buyer. If Buyer fails to cancel this Agreement within the Due Diligence Period, Buyer will be deemed to have waived the right to cancel under this section.

    B. PROPERTY INSPECTION/CONDITION: During the Due Diligence Period, Buyer shall take such action as Buyer deems necessary to determine whether the property is satisfactory to Buyer including, but not limited to, whether the property is insurable to Buyer's satisfaction, whether the property is insurable to Buyer's satisfaction, whether there are unsatisfactory conditions surrounding or otherwise affecting the Property; whether the Property is properly zoned. During such Period, Buyer shall have the right to have non-destructive inspection of all structural, roofing, mechanical, electrical, plumbing, heating/air conditioning, water/well/septic, pool/spa, survey, square footage, and any other property or systems, through licensed and bonded contractors or other qualified professionals. Seller agrees to provide reasonable access to the Property to Buyer and Buyer's inspections. Buyer agrees to indemnify and hold Seller harmless with respect to any injuries suffered by Buyer or third parties while on Seller's Property conducting such inspections, tests, or walk-throughs.

    C. CANCELLATION DUE TO INSPECTION REPORT: If Buyer cancels this Agreement due to a specific inspection report, Buyer shall provide Seller at the time of cancellation with a copy of the report containing the name, address, and telephone number of the inspector.

    D. PRELIMINARY TITLE REPORT: Within _____ business days of Opening of Escrow, Title Company _____ _____ shall provide Buyer with a Preliminary Title Report ("PTR") to review, which must be approved or rejected within _____ days of receipt thereof. If Buyer docs not object to the PTR within the period specified above, the PTR shall be deemed accepted. If Buyer makes any objection to any item(s) contained within the PTR, Seller shall have five (5) _____ business days after receipt of objections to correct or address the objections. If, within the time specified, Seller fails to have each such exception removed or to correct each such other matter as aforesaid, Buyer shall have the option to:

    1. Terminate this Agreement by providing notice to Seller and Escrow Officer, entitling Buyer to a refund of the EMD or

    2. Elect to accept title to the Property as is. All title exceptions approved or deemed accepted are hereafter collectively referred to as the "Permitted Exceptions."

    E. APPRAISAL: If the appraisal is less than the purchase price (1) Buyer, at Buyer's option, may pay the difference and purchase the Property for the Purchase Price, or (2) Seller, at Seller's option, may adjust the purchase price accordingly, such that the purchase price is equal to the appraisal, or (3) if the Parties cannot agree on option (1) or (2), either Party may cancel this Agreement upon written notice, in which event the EMD shall be returned to Buyer.

    F. FEDERAL FAIR HOUSING COMPLIANCE AND DISCLOSURES: Buyer is advised to consult with appropriate professional regarding neighborhood or Property conditions, including but not limited to: schools; proximity and adequacy of law services; existing and proposed transportation; construction and development; noise or odor from any source; and other nuisances, hazards, or circumstances. All properties are offered without regard to race, color, religion, sex, national origin, ancestry, handicap, or familial status and any other current requirements of federal fair housing law.

Each party acknowledges that he/she has read, understood, and agrees to each and every provision of this page unless a particular paragraph is otherwise modified by addendum or counteroffer.

        BUYER(S) INITIALS _____/_____   SELLER(S) INITIALS _____/_____

11. WALK-THROUGH INSPECTION OF PROPERTY: Buyer is entitled to a walk-through of the Property within _____ days prior to COE to ensure the Property and all major systems, appliances, heating/cooling, and electrical systems and mechanical fixtures are as stated in Seller's Real Property Disclosure Statement, and that the Property and improvements are in the same general condition as when this Agreement was signed by Seller and Buyer. To facilitate Buyer's walk-through, Seller is responsible for keeping all necessary utilities on. If any systems cannot be checked by Buyer on walk-through due to non-access or no power/gas/water, then Buyer reserves the right to hold Seller responsible for defects which could not be detected on walk-through because of lack of such access or power/gas/water. The purpose of the walk-through is to confirm (a) the Property is being maintained, (b) repairs, if any, have been completed as agreed, and (c) Seller has complied with Seller's other obligations.

12. CANCELLATION OF AGREEMENT: In the event this Agreement is properly cancelled in accordance with the terms contained herein, then Buyer will be entitled to a refund of the EMD.

13. ASSIGNMENT OF THIS AGREEMENT: Unless otherwise stated herein, this Agreement is non-assignable by Buyer without Seller's written consent.

14. RISK OF LOSS: If all or any material part of the Property is destroyed before transfer of legal title or possession, Seller cannot enforce the Agreement and Buyer is entitled to recover any portion of the sale price paid. If legal title or posession has transferred, risk of loss shall shift to Buyer.

15. DEFAULT:

A. IF BUYER DEFAULTS: If Buyer defaults in performance under this Agreement, Seller shall have one of the following legal recourses against Buyer (check one only):

☐ As Seller's sole legal recourse, Seller may retain, as liquidated damages, the EMD. In this respect, the Parties agree that Seller's actual damages would be difficult to measure and that the EMD is in fact a reasonable estimate of the damages that Seller would suffer as a result of Buyer's default,

☐ Seller shall have the right to recover from Buyer all of Seller's actual damages that Seller may suffer as a result of Buyer's default including, but not limited to, commissions due, expenses incurred until the Property is sold to a third party, and the difference in the sales price.

B. IF SELLER DEFAULTS: If Seller defaults in performance under this agreement, Buyer reserves all legal and/or equitable rights (such as specific performance) against Seller, and Buyer may seek to recover Buyer's actual damages incurred by Buyer due to Seller's default.

C. ESCROW: If this Agreement or any matter relating hereto shall become the subject of any litigation or controversy, Buyer and Seller agree, jointly and severally, to hold Escrow Holder free and harmless from any loss or expense, except losses or expenses as may arise from Escrow Holder's negligence or willful misconduct.

16. BROKER FEES: Buyer herein requires, and Seller agrees, as a condition of this Agreement, Seller will pay Listing Broker and Buyer's Broker, who becomes by this clause a third-party beneficiary to this Agreement, that certain sum or percentage of the purchase price (commission), that Seller, or Seller's Broker, offered for the procurement of ready, willing, and able Buyer via the Multiple Listing Service, any other advertisement or written offer. Seller understands and agrees that if Seller defaults hereunder, Buyer's Broker, as a third-party beneficiary of this Agreement, has the right to pursue all legal recourse against Seller for any commission due.

Each party acknowledges that he/she has read, understood, and agrees to each and every provision of this page unless a particular paragraph is otherwise modified by addendum or counteroffer.

BUYER(S) INITIALS _____/_____   SELLER(S) INITIALS _____/_____

17. WAIVER OF CLAIMS: Buyer and Seller agree that they are not relying upon any representations made by Brokers or Broker's agent. Buyer acknowledges that at COE, the Property will be sold AS-IS, WHERE-IS without any representations or warranties, unless expressly stated herein. Buyer agrees to satisfy himself as to the condition of the Property prior to COE. Buyer acknowledges that any statements of acreage or square footage by Brokers are simply estimates, and Buyer agrees to make such measurements, as Buyer deems necessary, to ascertain actual acreage or square footage. Buyer waives all claims against Brokers for (a) defects in the property; (b) inaccurate estimates of acreage or square footage; (c) environmental waste or hazards on the Property; (d) the fact that the Property may be in a flood zone; (e) the Property's proximity to freeways, airports, or other nuisances; (f) the zoning of the Property; (g) tax consequences; or (h) factors related to Buyer's failure to conduct walk-throughs, inspections, and research, as Buyer deems necessary.

18. DEFINITIONS:

Acceptance means the date that both parties have consented to and receipted a final, binding contract by affixing their signatures to this Agreement.

Agent means a licensee working under a Broker.

Agreement includes this document as well as all accepted counteroffers and addenda.

Buyer means one or more individuals or the entity that intends to purchase the Property.

Broker means the licensed real estate broker listed herein representing Seller and/or Buyer (and all real estate agents associated therewith).

COE means the date of recordation of the deed in Buyer's name.

EMD means Buyer's Earnest Money Deposit.

Escrow Holder means the neutral party that will handle the escrow.

PTR means Preliminary Title Report.

Property means the real property and any personal property included in the sale as provided herein.

Seller means one or more individuals or the entity that is the owner of the Property.

Title Company means the company that will provide title insurance.

19. MEDIATION: Before any legal action is taken to enforce any term or condition under this Agreement, the parties agree to engage in mediation, a dispute resolution process. Not withstanding the foregoing, in the event the buyer finds it necessary to file a claim for specific performance, this paragraph shall not apply.

Each party acknowledges that he/she has read, understood, and agrees to each and every provision of this page unless a particular paragraph is otherwise modified by addendum or counteroffer.

BUYER(S) INITIALS _____/_____   SELLER(S) INITIALS _____/_____

20. ADDITIONAL TERMS: _____

_____
_____
_____
_____
_____
_____
_____
_____
_____
_____
_____
_____
_____
_____
_____
_____
_____
_____
_____
_____
_____
_____
_____
_____
_____
_____

21. MISCELLANEOUS: Time is of the essence. No change, modification, or amendment of this Agreement shall be valid or binding unless such change, modification, or amendment shall be in writing and signed by each party. This Agreement will be binding upon the heirs, beneficiaries, and devisees of the parties hereto. This Agreement is executed in the State of _____, and the laws of that state shall govern its interpretation and effect. The parties agree that the county and state in which the Property is located is the appropriate forum for any action relating to this Agreement. Should any party hereto retain counsel for the purpose of initiating litigation to enforce or prevent the breach of any provision hereof, or for any other judicial remedy, then the prevailing party shall be entitled to be reimbursed by the losing party for all costs and expenses incurred thereby, including, but not limited to, reasonable attorneys fees and costs incurred by such prevailing party.

THIS IS A LEGALLY BINDING CONTRACT. All parties are advised to seek independent legal and tax advice to review the terms of this Agreement.

Each party acknowledges that he/she has read, understood, and agrees to each and every provision of this page unless a particular paragraph is otherwise modified by addendum or counteroffer.

BUYER(S) INITIALS _____/_____   SELLER(S) INITIALS _____/_____

BUYER'S OFFER

Upon Seller's acceptance, Buyer agrees to be bound by each provision of this Agreement, and all signed addenda, disclosures, and attachments. Unless this Agreement is accepted by execution below and delivered to the Buyer's Broker before the above date and time, this offer shall lapse and be of no further force and effect.

_____

Buyer's Full Name (print)   Buyer's Signature   Date   Time

_____

Buyer's Full Name (print)   Buyer's Signature   Date   Time

SELLER'S RESPONSE OFFER

Seller must respond by: _____ ☐AM ☐PM on (month) _____, (day) _____, 20_____.

EARNEST MONEY RECEIPT

Payment received by: _____

Amount $_____

Payment type: ☐ Cash

☐ Cashier's Check

☐ Personal Check

☐ Other _____

Upon acceptance, Earnest Money to be deposited within _____ business day(s), with:

☐ Escrow Holder

☐ Buyer's Broker's Trust Account

☐ Seller's Broker's Trust Account

Dated: _____ Signed: _____ Buyer's Agent

Each party acknowledges that he/she has read, understood, and agrees to each and every provision of this page unless a particular paragraph is otherwise modified by addendum or counteroffer.

BUYER(S) INITIALS _____/_____   SELLER(S) INITIALS _____/_____

□ **SELLER'S ACCEPTANCE**

ACCEPTANCE: Seller(s) acknowledges that he/she accepts and agrees to be bound by each provision of this Agreement, and all signed addenda, disclosures, and attachments.

□ **SELLER'S COUNTEROFFER**
Seller accepts the terms of this Agreement subject to the attached Counteroffer.

□ **SELLER'S REJECTION**
Seller hereby informs Buyer the presented herein is not accepted.

_____

Seller's Full Name (print)   Seller's Signature   Date   Time

_____

Seller's Full Name (print)   Seller's Signature   Date   Time

Each party acknowledges that he/she has read, understood, and agrees to each and every provision of this page unless a particular paragraph is otherwise modified by addendum or counteroffer.

BUYER(S) INITIALS _____/_____   SELLER(S) INITIALS _____/_____

COUNTEROFFER

AGENT NAME: _____

COMPANY NAME: _____

☐ Offer ☐ Counteroffer	Made by: ☐ Seller ☐ Buyer
To ☐ Buy ☐ Sell the real property commonly known as:	Name:

_____ dated _____ is not accepted in its current form, but the following Counteroffer is hereby submitted:

OTHER TERMS: All other terms remain the same as the original Offer and Acceptance plus terms agreed to in Counteroffer(s) No. _____.

EXPIRATION: This Counteroffer shall expire unless a copy hereof with ☐ Buyer's ☐ Seller's written acceptance is delivered to ☐ Buyer ☐ Seller or his Agent by: _____.

Date: _____

_____
☐ Buyer ☐ Seller   Signature

Time: _____

_____
☐ Buyer ☐ Seller   Signature

The undersigned ☐ Buyer ☐ Seller hereby: _____ accepts the Counteroffer — or — _____ rejects the Counteroffer.

Date: _____

_____
☐ Buyer ☐ Seller   Signature

Time: _____

_____
☐ Buyer ☐ Seller   Signature

ADDENDUM TO PURCHASE AGREEMENT

In reference to Agreement of Sale executed by _____
_____, as Buyer(s), dated _____, _____, covering the real property
commonly known as _____

It is further agreed by both parties as follows:

This agreement, upon its execution by both parties, is herewith made an integral part of the aforementioned agreement of sale. When properly completed this is a binding contract.

The undersigned Buyer, having inspected the above described property and its appurtenance, offers and agress to purchase said property on the terms and conditions herein stated and acknowledges receipt of a copy of this agreement from the Agent.

_____   _____
BUYER   DATE/TIME

_____   _____
BUYER   DATE/TIME

ACCEPTANCE OF OFFER TO PURCHASE
The undersigned Seller accepts the foregoing offer to purchase and agrees to sell the above described property on the terms and conditions as stated herein and acknowledges receipt of a copy of this agreement.

_____   _____
SELLER   DATE/TIME

_____   _____
SELLER   DATE/TIME

_____   _____
AUTHORIZED AGENT   PHONE

AFFIDAVIT OF TITLE TO OBTAIN LOAN

I, _____, being sworn, depose and say:

I reside at _____ and am the owner in fee simple of the following described premises: _____.

The premises have been in my possession since _____ [Date] that my possession has been peaceable and undisturbed, and the title has never been disputed, questioned, or rejected, nor insurance refused, as far as I know. I know of no facts by reason of which the possession or title might be called in question, or by reason of which any claim to any part of the premises or any interest in it adverse to me might be set up. There are no judgments against me unpaid or unsatisfied of record entered in any court of this state, or of the United States, and the premises are, as far as I know, free from all leases, mortgages, taxes, assessments, charges, and other liens and encumbrances, except _____.

The premises are now occupied by _____.

No proceedings in bankruptcy have ever been initiated by, or against me in any court or before any officer of any state, or of the United States, nor have I at any time made an assignment for the benefit of creditors, nor an assignment, now in effect, of the rents of the premises or any part of it.

I am a citizen of the United States, and am more than _____ years old. I am by occupation _____.

I am married to _____, who is over _____ years of age and is competent to convey or mortgage real estate. I was married to _____ on _____ [Date]. I have never been married to any other person now living. I have not been known by any other name during the past _____ years.

There are no actions pending affecting the described premises. No repairs, alterations, or improvements have been made to the premises which have not been completed more than _____ days prior to the date of this affidavit. There are no facts known to me relating to the title to the premises which have not been set forth in this affidavit.

This affidavit is made to induce _____ to make a loan to me in the amount of $_____, to be secured by a mortgage on the premises.

Sworn and subscribed before me _____ [Date].

BANK COMMITMENT LETTER

National Bank of _____

[Date]

In response to your request for a loan of _____ to acquire, renovate, and equip the facilities at _____ in _____, we are pleased to offer _____ Corporation the following:

Amount: _____

Terms: The rate of interest shall be a fixed rate of _____ for _____ years. Payments of _____ shall be due and payable on or before the first day of each and every month for _____ consecutive months beginning on the first day of the month next succeeding the closing.

Fees: The bank shall charge and collect at the time of closing a closing fee of _____ percent of the principal amount of the loan. This fee shall be in addition to any interest charged on the loan.

Collateral: This loan shall be secured by a first mortgage lien in the amount of _____ on the premises acquired and renovated at _____ Avenue. In addition, the bank shall receive security in the form of a security interest (UCC-1 Financing Statement) in the amount of _____ on all personal property located at _____ Avenue. Neither the mortgage nor the security interest shall be subject to any prior liens. In addition, the bank shall receive a second mortgage lien on the real and personal property of the residence at _____ in _____, of which _____ and _____ are mortgagors.

Guarantee: An unconditional personal guarantee shall be required from _____ _____ and _____.

Conditions: The company shall obtain subordinated mortgage financing commitments in the amount of _____ from the _____ Economic Development Commission. The financing shall be for a period of _____ years.

This commitment represents the maximum loan amount the bank will provide for this project.

BANK COMMITMENT LETTER (CONTINUED)

In addition to the above commitment, the bank is willing to advance interim. In addition to the above commitment, the bank is willing to advance interim financing in the amount not to exceed _____ at a rate of _____ for _____ months provided the borrower submits satisfactory evidence and assignments of commitment from subordinated mortgage lenders totalling _____.

This commitment shall remain in effect to _____ [Date], if this commitment is accepted by the borrower by signing and returning to the bank a copy of this letter by _____ [Date]. In the event that there is any material adverse change in the company's financial condition or obligations prior to the closing, the bank may, at its sole and complete discretion, terminate this commitment.

Accepted	Sincerely
Borrower	
	Senior Credit Administrator
	National Bank of

Date _____

If you have an adjustable-rate mortgage and the fixed-rate period is over, refinancing is recommended because your interest rate is now free to rise.

INDEX

BIBLIOGRAPHY and REFERENCES

Bibliography

McClean, Andrew, The home Buyers Advisor

Glink, Ilyce R., 100 Questions Every First Time Home Buyer Should Ask, second edition, Random House

Irwin, Robert, Buy Your First Home, third edition, Deaborn Trade Publishing

Philbin, Tom, How to hire a home improvement contractor without being chiseled, a991 St. Martin's Press

Heldmann Carl, Be your Own house contractor, third edition, Storey Communications, Inc

Gallaty, Allaway, Kyle, Modern real estate practice, 16th edition, Deaborn Real Estate Education

Glink, Ilyce R., 10 steps to Home Ownership, A workbook for first time home buyers, Random House

References

American School of Mortgage Banking
www.bankofamerica.com
www.abanet.org
www.srqmls.com
www.ginnimae.gov
www.fanniemae.com
www.freddiemac.com
www.hud.gov
www.namb.org
www.remax.com
www.hsh.com
www.asaonline.org

MORE GREAT TITLES FROM ATLANTIC PUBLISHING

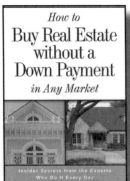
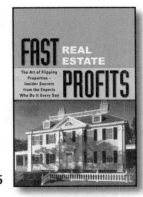

MORE GREAT TITLES FROM ATLANTIC PUBLISHING

THE REAL ESTATE INVESTOR'S HANDBOOK: THE COMPLETE GUIDE FOR THE INDIVIDUAL INVESTOR

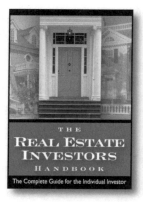

This book is a must-have for beginning investors, real estate veterans, commercial brokers, sellers, and buyers. This comprehensive step-by-step proven program shows beginners and seasoned veterans alike the ins and outs of real estate investing. This book is a road map to successful investing in real estate. Real estate appreciates at a rate far greater than the rate of inflation, builds equity, provides a steady return on investment, provides cash flow, and can offer substantial tax benefits. This handbook is the resource for novices and pros alike; it will guide you through every step of the process of real estate investing. You will uncover secrets that expert real estate investors use every day. This comprehensive resource contains a wealth of modern tips and strategies for getting started in this very lucrative area.

432 Pages • Item # RIH-02 • $24.95

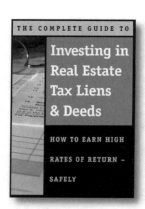

THE COMPLETE GUIDE TO INVESTING IN REAL ESTATE TAX LIENS & DEEDS: HOW TO EARN HIGH RATES OF RETURN—SAFELY

Tax lien certificates and deeds are not purchased through a broker; you purchase these property tax liens directly from the state or county government (depending on the state). Investing in tax liens and deeds can be very rewarding. Tax liens can be tax deferred or even tax-free. You can purchase them in your self-directed IRA. Interest rates vary but average between 4% and 18%. The interest rates are fixed by local governments, essentially a government-guaranteed loan. This sounds great, but you must know what you are doing! This groundbreaking book will provide everything you need to know to get you started on generating high-investment returns with low risk, from start to finish.

288 Pages • Item # CGI-02 • $21.95

THE RENTAL PROPERTY MANAGER'S TOOLBOX— A COMPLETE GUIDE INCLUDING PRE-WRITTEN FORMS, AGREEMENTS, LETTERS, AND LEGAL NOTICES: WITH COMPANION CD-ROM

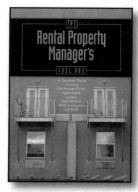

This book and will teach you how to professionally manage your rental property. Maximize your profits and minimize your risks. Learn about advertising, tenants, legal rights, landlord rights, discrimination, vacancies, essential lease clauses, crime prevention, security issues, as well as premises liability, security deposits, handling problems, evictions, maintenance, recordkeeping, and taxes. The CD-ROM contains dozens of forms, sample contracts and more.

288 Pages • Item # RPM-02 • $29.95 with Companion CD-ROM

To order call 1-800-814-1132 or visit www.atlantic-pub.com